To Robert P. Bray
from Theressa L. Cro[...]

MEETING THE CHALLENGE

MEETING THE CHALLENGE

Your Invitation to Enter the Turbulent Years of Adulthood

Herbert C. Gabhart

BROADMAN PRESS
Nashville, Tennessee

Unless otherwise noted, all Scripture quotations are from the King James Version of the Bible.

Scripture quotations marked (Centenary) are from *The New Testament in Modern English,* Centenary Translation by Helen Barrett Montgomery. Copyright © 1924 by Judson Press. Used by permission of Judson Press.

Library of Congress Cataloging in Publication Data

Gabhart, Herbert C., 1914-
   Meeting the challenge.

   Summary: Discusses the uniqueness of the individual,
God's highest creation; the purpose of life and the
direction it should take; and opportunities and how to
pursue them.
   1. Youth—Conduct of life. 2. Youth—Religious life.
[1. Conduct of life] I. Title.
BJ1661.G23 1984   248.8'3   83-71398
ISBN 0-8054-5340-7

PRESENTED

TO

_____

BY

_____

_____

Place

_____

Date

Introduction

I think I know how I could start a lengthy discussion in any group. All I would need to do is ask, Which is the most important six-year period in a person's life? There would be takers at each station of life. Some would say that a six-year period is not a wise division length. Others would say that it is not possible to divide life into stages, as did Shakespeare in *As You Like It*, and that all the world is not a stage where men and women are merely players with their acts being seven ages.

The fact remains, however, that we do tend to divide life into segments from the standpoint of growth, age, training, and experiences. I would say that the most important six-year period in an individual's life covers years sixteen through twenty-two. Two-thirds of my life has been spent with individuals who are going through that period and working with persons like you who are facing the challenge of these years.

Age sixteen through twenty-two is a crucial time in your life. It is an exciting time. It is a significant time. It is a rewarding time. It is a fast-moving track with varieties of experiences. There's rarely a dull moment. You find in yourself an element of daring as well as an element of nonchalance. It is a period packed with changes, stuffed with decisions, bulging with events, and stacked with opportunities.

You leave old friends and make new ones. You depart the familiar scenes centering around home and live in tents located either in the wilderness of the far country or in the promised land of academe! Going from the junior and senior years of high school where status has been attained among one's peers into an environment of new faces and new surroundings is somewhat traumatic. The campus is so different from the high school grounds.

College days are days of preparation for profession. No longer are your decisions either made or strongly suggested by parents. You are basically on your own. You've cut the ties to Mom's apron string. A new experience of independence comes quickly. There is no one to demand that homework be done. No one to call, "It's time to get up," each morning. No one to wait up at night to tuck you into bed. Decisions have to be made alone, sometimes quickly and without recourse.

These years are significant from the standpoint of friendships. It's likely that you will meet your husband- or wife-to-be during these years.

Someone once remarked that it is during these years that "youth is climbing fool's hill." There is no other way to mature than to climb this arduous, rugged, treacherous hill. Doubts assail many young persons climbing the hill. Doubts relating to religious faith, the meaning of life, and the worthwhileness of it all keep assaulting the climber. Very few, if any, are totally prepared for this experience.

Many like you make a mad dash in search of the fabled El Dorado, the perennial fountain of youth, and the easy road of least resistance. While on their new-found "ownness" they want to ride off madly in every direction. If possible, many want to spend their weeks sowing wild oats and then go to church occasionally to pray for a crop failure.

All of this has produced a situation which some call a communication gap between youth and parents. You just don't seem to be on the same wave length. While all of this may be painful for both you and your parents, it can be a positive experience. As you grow and mature, you will leave the dependencies of childhood. These years following high school can do a lot toward setting the course of your life as an adult. You can continue to put away childish things. Some days you will feel that you have arrived at maturity. You don't want advice from anybody. Other days you will wish you could be a child again. The responsibilities of adulthood, the decisions you are called upon to make, will seem much bigger than you.

Moving through these years of transition is like steering through white water rapids. It will take all you have and more. And you have a lot. God has blessed you and your generation with opportunities no other generation has had. You have traveled and experienced more than any previous generation.

You have within you an idealism that can stand you in good stead as you face the realities of life. Your frankness and dislike of phoniness will serve you well. Your mind contains potential that you will tap only a portion of in your whole life.

Steering through the rapids of these years is *your* task. No one can do this for you. This doesn't mean that you are alone. God is with you in all circumstances. There are many people who care about your journey—more people than you realize. Your journey through the rapids can be easier when you realize that there are people pulling for you, shouting encouragement from the banks. Many of these have been through the same rapids you are going through. Talking to them can help you know where there are obstructions near the surface, as well as where there are strong depth currents to be aware of.

I have been through these rapids. I have watched with interest and care many people like you make this portion of their journey through life. I offer this book with a prayer that yours may be a rewarding journey and with confidence that you will meet the challenge.

Contents

Acknowledgments

I wish to thank very sincerely my wife, Helen, whose love and wisdom have been such a vital part of my life during the past forty years of togetherness; to our three daughters, Diana, Betty, and Jo Ellen, as all have happily met the challenge; and to the thousands of students who have come through Belmont College during my twenty-three years as president. Also, I am grateful and appreciative of my secretary, Elsie Humphreys, for her invaluable assistance.

Section I
Who Am I?

You couldn't have asked a more profound or appropriate question. It strikes at the center of things. You are not an orphan of the apes left on a hostile planet to fend for yourself without a beneficent Heavenly Father. You are not just a little animal living precariously on a second-rate planet attached to a second-rate star. You are a very unusual creature with unusual features and an unusual potential. It really is hard to comprehend what all you are and especially who you are.

I think, however, we will find it very interesting, and hopefully very helpful, to take a look at the various ingredients that comprise human beings.

Biologically you are a vertebrate animal of the class *Mammalia* with certain distinguishing characteristics. Those characteristics are: your body is covered by hair; you are possessed of mammary glands. You are also of the class *Homo Sapiens* which goes a step further and attributes to you mental capabilities; but sometimes an individual will, through laziness and carelessness, fall into the class designated "Homo Ignoramus."

The Greeks had a word for man, *Anthropos,* which carried with it the idea that man was a creature with a divine kinship giving him an upward look. You are more than "a tale told by an idiot, full of sound and fury, signifying nothing." You are more than "a sick fly taking a dizzy ride on a giant Ferris wheel."

It is so easy in our electronic age to think of a person as a digit in a decimal system or a code number. Not too many years ago we inaugurated a rule in the finance office of the college that all returned checks would carry a $1.00 penalty. One day the

13

cashier said to me, "You owe the college a $1.00 because one of your checks was returned from the bank."

This shocked me somewhat because I knew that there were sufficient funds on deposit to cover the check. Upon looking at the slip attached to the check, I noticed that the reason given for rejection was that I had omitted my code number. At the bank I was that code number, not a person. We are aware that it is important to remember certain code numbers—our Social Security number, and hopefully our telephone number. I am sure that I, and I think you also, do not wish to be called by a number. We much prefer to have our names called.

Our names designate in one respect who we are family-wise. You are the child of your parents. They conceived you and gave you birth. They cared for you during your infant days and provided love, nourishment, and a place to romp and sleep. It is important for you to remember your birthdate and have a birth certificate. You are a part of your parents, your grandparents, and great-grandparents. These are your family connections.

But you are more. You are a distinct person, unlike your parents, even though there is strong similarity. You are different from any of the 3.5 billion living persons today and different from any of the 67 billions who have walked the earth from the beginning until this present generation. There has never been one like you, and there never will be another like you. You are unique—one of a kind.

You are possessed with the power of choice. You are not a robot, a marionette, or a puppet. You can choose. You do not have to blindly obey anyone or anything. You can choose right or wrong, good or bad, bitter or sweet. In this respect, you are superior to angels. Angels don't have the power of choice. They obey only the voice of God. In order to assist you in making and handling your choices, you are possessed with a dual system: a power system comprised of passion, purpose, energy, muscle, heartbeat and a control system to keep the power system from running recklessly in all directions. Your control system is comprised of conscience, will, conviction, religious commitment, and your sense of values.

You are a unique, important person. You are the only animal that walks upright. You can stand erect, tall. You are the greatest miracle in the world. I say that without reservation. You are the only animal that can laugh, reason, plan for the future and eternity. You are the only animal that can drive a car, soar 35,000 feet or more into the ethereal blue. You are the only animal that can create beyond mere instinct. You are capable of great wonders, capable of putting those wonders in color on a canvas for others to enjoy.

Even in jest we tend to augment our distinctive human features. It has been said about humans that they are the only animal that can be skinned more than once and still live. We are the only animal who makes bargains, trades wares. We are the only animal that cooks food.

You are also a paradox and a partnership. You are a paradox of dust and divinity, both animalistic at times and God-like at other times. You are also both greatness and misery. Your partnership consists of your visible self and the invisible spirit of your Maker.

In working within the paradox and functioning as one of the partners, you may assume three roles: the person you are, the person you would like to be, and the person you ought to be.

As we try to think through the rapids of the years sixteen through twenty-two, we will touch base time and time again with our concept of who we are.

There is a striking line in Eugene O'Neill's fantastic play *The Great God Brown*. When the central figure, Brown, lies dead on the street, a policeman bends over his body and asks, "Well, what's his name?"

Someone replies, "Man."

Then the policeman, with notebook and pencil demands, "How do you spell it?"[1]

That is the major question: How do you spell human? What does it mean? The correct spelling is not that humans are a chemical accident or the most intelligent of the apes, but "Now are we the sons of God" (1 John 3:2).

In order to get a fuller concept of who you are, let us look at these five affirmations in the following chapters: You Are a Unique Biological Creature; You Are Endowed with a Remarkable Mind; You Are Possessed of a Living Soul; You Are a Vital Part of Society; You Have a Growing Shadow.

Note

1. Halford E. Luccock, *Marching Off the Map* (New York: Harper and Brothers, 1952), p. 72.

1

You Are
a Unique Biological Creature

You have a wonderful, beautiful body. It is yours to nurture, groom, and preserve. No one has one just like yours.

The reason I have said that you have a wonderful, beautiful body is because God in the beginning created all things. His crowning act was creating humans, and after he had finished with his acts of creation he said, "Behold, it was very good" (Gen. 1:31). We are the most marvelous thing in existence. Nothing that we have created comes close to the marvels of the human body. No computer, no machine, no building, no robot—nothing can compare with the marvelous versatility of the human body.

How could a person be an atheist after considering the structure of the human body—the coherence of the parts and the great wear, resistance, and repairability of those parts? When I was a lad, I would frequently fall and skin my knees. With blood dripping from the torn flesh, I would go to my father and show him what had happened. He would look at the wound, pour on some turpentine, and then say, "Well, Son, that will heal and repair itself. Did you tear your breeches?" His inference was that the flesh would take care of itself, but the trousers I had on were not capable of self-repair. Mom would have to repair my clothing. My clothes were man made while my body was created by God.

Dr. Alexis Carrel, in his book *Man the Unknown*, says, "The human body is placed, on the scale of magnitudes, halfway between the atom and the star. According to the size of the objects selected for comparison, it appears either large or small.

Its length is equivalent to that of two hundred thousand tissue cells, or of two millions of ordinary microbes, or of two billions of albumin molecules, placed end to end. Man is gigantic in comparison with an electron, an atom, a molecule, or a microbe. But, when compared with a mountain, or with the earth, he is tiny. More than four thousand individuals would have to stand one upon the other in order to equal the height of Mount Everest."[1]

Shakespeare remarked:

> What a piece of work man is:
> How noble in reason
> How infinite in faculty
> In form and moving, how express and admirable
> In action, how like an angel
> In apprehension, how like a god.[2]

Let us take a look at the body of this unusual creature that can act at times like a roaring lion, like a thieving fox or like a rapacious vulture, while at other times can act like a gentle, ardent lover, a good Samaritan, and a compassionate brother.

The human body is comprised of nine components: the basic unit cell, central nervous system, sensory organs, glands, circulatory system, digestive system, reproductive organs, urinary tract, and structural system of bones.[3]

It would be impossible to look at each of the nine components. I have chosen to comment briefly upon the brain, the eye, the heart, and the hand.

Your *brain* weighs only about three pounds, or one-fiftieth of the average person's weight. It resides just above a person's eyes in the top of his head. It has about 30 billion neurons and five to ten times that number of cells. Each of the 30 billion nerve cells connects with other cells, some as many as 60,000 times. Once a brain cell is lost it cannot be replaced, while skin and blood cells can be replaced. The brain handles all the stimuli traffic during waking and sleeping hours. It stores knowledge, facts, and feelings. It has been estimated that if a person were to build a building to duplicate the work of the human brain it would be larger than Rockefeller Center in New York and that if one were to cool the brain with a synthetic air conditioner one would need to divert the waters of the Hudson River.

Your *eyes* make about 70,000 color photographs daily while the brain files those pictures. Just think of what that much film would cost today. No larger than a Ping-Pong ball, the eye has tens of millions of electrical connections and can handle a million or more simultaneous messages. Through the eye gate comes 80 percent of our knowledge. The eyes are connected to the brain by 300,000 separate and private "telephone" lines. When you look at a vase of flowers, thousands of separate messages are rapidly sent to the brain, telling the size, color, shape, and smell of the flowers. Tears wash your eyes with nature's strongest germ killer. Your eyes are powerfully expressive. The eyes, through blinking, can suggest warmth, anger, or affection. In twinkling the eye suggests kindness, enthusiasm, and joy.

The story is told of a chemistry professor who once mixed the wrong solutions in the laboratory and the aftermath of the explosion which followed left the professor with one eye destroyed. In consultation with his doctor, the doctor told the professor that he could put a glass eye in the socket to replace the destroyed eye and that he could match perfectly the good eye. "Well and good," said the professor. "But, Doc, there is one stipulation. You must put a twinkle in the glass eye."

Your *heart* weighs only about twelve ounces. It is red-brown in color and is about six inches long and four inches wide, pear shaped, and poetically referred to as being romantic in character. In a day the heart will pump twenty-five pounds of blood through 60,000 miles of blood vessels. That is enough pumping to fill a 4,000-gallon tank car and enough energy to raise a 165-pound man 2,500 feet into the air. In doing this, the heart will beat 103,689 times a day, resting 16 hours and working 8 hours. The heart works day and night and gets blamed for fatigue, dizziness, and various maladies. It expresses itself by responding to affection, feeling, and exercise.

Your *hands* are marvelous instruments. They are a part of your structural system. Basically, hands are pieces of machinery: an array of levers, hinges, and a source of power managed by the brain. The hand is comprised of a total of twenty-seven bones, fifty-four in the two hands, for more than a fourth of all the bones in the body. The hands are very maneuverable. With hands you can type, play a piano, make a fist, lift objects, and feel for things. If your eyes were gone, you could read through your hands by learning braille. If deaf, you could speak by using sign language. Extraordinary things can be done with the hands.

Now, in light of the marvelous structure of your wonderful, beautiful body, let us ponder four very important questions.

First, how tall should a person be? We live in a tall world. Buildings are going higher and higher. People on the whole are growing taller and taller. If you don't believe this, compare the height of today's professional basketball teams with those of three or four decades ago. But I don't want to focus your attention on physical height. That is really not too significant. Tallness and smallness of stature both have their compensating factors.

What I am concerned about are physical ideas of heights cast into the context of spiritual dimensions. The Philistine giant Goliath, conquered by David, may have been one of the tallest persons ever to live, but there have been many spiritual giants whose physical dimensions could not match the giant's measurements. Maybe the true measurement of a person is not from the sole of the foot to the top of the head, but the size of his heart.

I believe a person should be able to stand on tiptoes and pluck the ripe apples from the orchards of history. My major professor said, "You never understand anything until you understand it historically. For history is His Story, God working with and through persons." A tall person is one who has plucked the lessons of history. There are several of those lessons: "Whom the gods would destroy, they first make mad." "A bee stings a flower to fertilize it." "It is usually darkest before the dawn." "Truth crushed to earth shall rise again, the eternal years of God are hers while Error writhes in pain and dies among his worshipers."

I believe a person should be tall enough to reach out with his arms and pull a world 25,000 miles in circumference close to his heart. In Greek mythology Atlas held the world on his shoulders, but the tall person of today needs to hold the world in his heart.

I believe a person should be tall enough to rise above the clouds of envy, strife, greed, and mediocrity to occasionally bump the stars. A person does not need to walk with her head in the clouds; she needs to walk with her head through the clouds, free of earthbound self-gratification and self-centeredness.

And lastly, I believe a person should be tall enough to reach heaven's threshold of blessings while on bended knees in arduous petition to the Keeper of those blessings. Never count a person out who is kneeling in prayer. God and persons together form an unbeatable team. History says that Mary Stuart, queen of Scotland, once remarked that she feared the prayers of John Knox more than ten thousand soldiers.

My *second question* is this: *What are your dimensions?* We have discussed heights; now let us look at other dimensions of the human being. What size shoe do you wear? Oh, that is really not the issue. I am thinking of your ability to stand firm for the things that count. I am thinking of your capability in the direction of scaling the unknown heights. I am thinking of the foundation support upon which your life is based.

What is the size of your hands? Some athletes have very big hands. Other people have slender, graceful hands. What can you hold in your hands? A cup of cold water for a thirsty friend. A gentle caress for a discouraged friend. Are you able to seize the opportunities that everywhere abound? Can you hold on when hope is gone?

How big is your head? In some lingo bigheadedness is very undesirable. It suggests the idea of conceit, egotism, and self-pride. But I am thinking of a head which is capable of holding an interest and concern for those things that are high and holy. I am thinking of a head big enough to contain ounces of gratitude.

Gratitude is a vanishing virtue. Ingratitude could be one of the worst of sins. A lady got on a city bus that was crowded. There were no vacant seats. A gentleman got up and offered the lady his seat. She fainted. When she revived she said, "Thank you, sir," and he fainted. That may be a rather extreme illustration of the paucity of gratefulness, but it does appropriately illustrate my point. Is your head big enough to remember kind deeds and seek to do another a similar kindness?

How big is your heart? Does it contain the hurts, injustices, and sufferings of the world? Is it just big enough for your friends? Is it big enough and full enough to give away love, peace, and joy? Is it big enough to accept the truth that red and yellow, black and white, all are precious in the good Lord's sight?

Your body contains 202 bones. Without these bones you would fall flat on your face. Bones give form to the human body. It would be of little value to study the human body without considering the function of the various parts of the body. Someone has rather cleverly written a poem entitled "Which Bone Are You?" The essence of the poem centers around four types of people designated by using the word *bone* in each group. I would like my *third question* to be "*Which Bone Are You?*"[4]

Wishbone People
They hope for, they long for,
They wish for and sigh;
They want things to come, but
Aren't willing to try.

These persons are those who spend time at the wishing wells. They put teeth under their pillows waiting for the visit of the fairies. They frequent the fountain of youth. They are always looking for a ship to come in that hasn't even been sent out. They expect the wheel of chance to come up with their number or that a rich, unknown uncle might die leaving them the bulk of his estate. These persons accomplish little in life.

Funny Bone People
They laugh, grin and giggle,
Twinkle the eye,
If work is a joke, sure they'll
Give it a try!

This group spends time eating, drinking, and making merry. They want to be entertained. They want their funny bones tickled. They do not want to take things seriously; in fact, they avoid the tough and the untried.

Jawbone People
They scold, paw and splutter,
They froth, rave and cry;
They are long on the talk, but
They are short on try.

These are the people who have never learned that silence can be either golden or yellow and that we need to know the difference. These are the people who have not learned the biblical admonitions, "Let your speech be alway with grace, seasoned with salt, that ye may know how ye ought to answer every man" (Col. 4:6), and "A word fitly spoken is like apples of gold in pictures of silver" (Prov. 25:11).

Backbone People
They strike from the shoulder,
They never say die;
They are the winners in life, for they
Know how to try.

What a group are the backbone people! They are the ones who press forward. They run patiently and enduringly. They count the cost and tackle the job with fervor. They look for opportunity instead of security.

In meeting the challenge, I would suggest that you become a "backbone" person. You are equipped to make the choice.

My *fourth question* is this: *Can you manufacture spizzerinctum within your body? Spizzerinctum* is a good word. It is in your dictionary. It means: "get up and git," "second-mile energy," "drive," and "enthusiastic push." All of the ingredients are within your body for success. Mediocrity is self-inflicted. It is estimated that if humans could develop fully their energy potential and that energy could be sold at the same rate of a kilowatt measure of energy, a 165-pound person would be worth 85.5 billion dollars. Chemically, a person is worth only about $5.00. The potential is in each of us. It must be fed with desire, longing, vision, ambition. Spizzerinctum will prevent a person who may have failed from having contentment with that failure. It will cause a person to get out of bed and get to the job on time. It will cause him, while on the job, to perform to his maximum.

Henry Wadsworth Longfellow described, in his *Ladder of Saint Augustine,* great men who must have been spizzerinctum manufacturers when he penned these words:

> The heights by great men reached and kept
> Were not attained by sudden flight,
> But they, while their companions slept,
> Were toiling upward in the night.

You do have a wonderful, beautiful body loaded with tremendous potential. You are a rarity. Develop and protect your body for you are one of a kind. You will never have but one you. You would never think of putting sand in the mechanism of your watch, nor would you put gravel in the gas tank of your car, so be careful what goes into that wonderful body of yours. Treat it with respect. Do not malign it.

One day at our Kiwanis Club, a Marine Corps recruiter was addressing the group and stated that so many of the young people today were unable to pass the physical test in order to get into the US Marine Corps. When asked what he attributed the cause of so many failures, he replied, "Too much junk food and too many soft drinks." I was surprised, but on second thought I understood what he was saying. Young people are not eating right. They are not giving themselves balanced meals.

Eat properly, your wonderful body demands that. Sleep

adequately so that your wonderful body can repair itself. Exercise abundantly so that your muscles will be properly toned. "Know ye not that [your body is] the temple of God, and that the Spirit of God dwelleth in you?" (1 Cor. 3:16).

Count your blessings. Take the long look. Live to your maximum. Respect your body; honor its needs. Your body is a marvelous machine. Take care of it. It can be a strong ally as you face and meet the challenge.

Notes

1. Alexis Carrel, *Man, the Unknown* (New York: Harper and Brothers, 1935), p. 60.
2. Shakespeare, *Hamlet*, II, 2ii, Line 315.
3. J. D. Ratcliff, *Your Body and How It Works,* pp. ix-xi: *Contents of the Body:* 1. The Basic Unit: cell; 2. Central Nervous System: brain, hypothalamus; 3. Sensory Organs: eye, ear, nose, skin, tongue; 4. Glands of Internal Secretion: pituitary, thyroid, thymus, adrenal; 5. Circulatory System: heart, lung, bloodstream; 6. Digestive System: eyetooth, throat, stomach, intestine, liver, pancreas; 7. Reproductive Organs: womb, ovary, breast, testis; 8. Urinary Tract: kidney, bladder, prostate; 9. Structural and Other Body Components: spine, foot, hand, hair
4. "Which Bone Are You?" author unknown.

2

You Are Endowed with a Remarkable Mind

Your IQ, ACT, or SAT test scores may or may not suggest just how remarkable is your mind. It is unquestionably endowed with an indescribable capacity. There is nothing quite like the human mind from the standpoint of capability, capacity for work, and the ease with which it stores and recalls fact.

Your mind is your kingdom. Chaucer said, "My mind to me a kingdom is; such present joys therein I find, that it excels all other bliss that earth affords." He was right a thousandfold. Your mind is your kingdom, and you are the ruling king over that kingdom.

Ardis Whitman, in his book *A New Image of Man*, tells about a cartoon published several years ago in an issue of *Time* in which a psychiatrist, feet braced and brow furrowed, fished into the open top of a patient's head. "With evident satisfaction he yanked from it an enormous pile of cluttered junk. Freudian symbols from eyes to watches piled ankle deep around him and it was only when the poor woman's skull was almost empty that the operation was declared successful." And Whitman concluded most appropriately, "This is not far from what most of us believe—that the brain is an understandable and smoothly functioning instrument whenever it is not cluttered with the waste of bad thoughts, complexes, fixations, and that such unwanted intruders can almost literally be extracted like a tooth, leaving everything working smoothly again."[1]

The mind is so remarkable that its potential and capabilities are frequently overlooked due to the fact that it is involved in every activity of every day. We tend to take its growth and expansion for granted. According to scientists, the brain will handle ten billion impressions in a lifetime and the average person will not use more than one-fourth of the mind's capability. If that estimate is correct, it is high time that we get serious about our minds.

Milton expressed a verifiable truth in strong terms when he said, "The mind is its own place, and in itself can make a heaven of hell and a hell of heaven."[2]

What then is that thing we call *mind*? Let us look at it from at least five standpoints, and these are not listed in priority order because who among us could establish a priority of mental activities?

The mind assimilates and stores facts, ideas, information, and feelings. Its storage capacity is almost limitless. Probably no person who has ever lived has been able to use all the storage space in the mind. No computer ever invented can handle as much information or as many facts as the developed mind. And incidentally, whenever the mind chooses to recall a fact, it can do so without any screeching of file drawers or whir of machinery. It does so silently and smoothly. Almost coincidentally with the recall of any fact or idea is an accompanying feeling piggybacked on the fact.

Recently, my wife and I were driving to Knoxville, Tennessee. We were cruising along the Cumberland Plateau near Crossville when she began to sing, "Oh, the Hatfields and the McCoys, they were reckless mountain boys . . ."

I asked, "What made you burst forth with that song?"

"Guess," she asked. There was no way I could find a clue. Then she let me in on her secret. She had seen a highway sign with the name of a nearby city, Jamestown. She has a friend who has a friend living in Jamestown with the name *Hatfield*. When the name *Hatfield* came into her mind, she immediately thought of the song, "The Hatfields and the McCoys." Being a native West Virginian might have helped, but the mind quickly and silently put it all in place until she gave expression to the song.

How does this work? Well, no one knows.

The mind is the generator and director of action. Whenever a fearful and dangerous scene comes into the mind through the eye gate there is an immediate response. The body quickly prepares for action. The glands come immediately to attention, reporting for duty, and the other capacity centers of the mind in a split second, like high-level conferences, determine some course of action.

The mind provides an interpreter. The cry of a child in the middle of the night, coming through the ear gate of the sleeping parent, is quickly translated into a sense of need, demanding immediate attention from the parent. The mind makes that immediate interpretation of need and stirs the loving parent into action. Spoken words are meaningless sounds until the mind identifies those sounds as having rememberable meaning, or let us take another illustration. Suppose the phone rings, and the voice on the other end of the line is the voice of a loved one not heard for months. What happens? Instantly the mind creates an image of the loved one, a recognition of the loved one's voice, and a flood of memories and questions await their turn for recognition.

The mind is a refinery of reason, logic, and thought. It has the capability of making value judgments. It has the capability to rationalize and draw conclusions. It can, through memory, put all the facts and features previously stored away into the conscious realm of consideration. Additionally, it can gather together all relevant matters and suggest a logical approach to the issue in question.

The mind is the tailor of attitudes. Attitudes are so important in life. They tend to determine one's altitude. Negative attitudes are drab and very harmful while positive attitudes add color and light to life. An attitude is the way one looks at something. It is a feeling. It is a mood. It helps determine the position taken on a matter by an individual.

It is very imperative that one who wishes to have a strong, clean mind spend time developing and educating the conscience, that sense of right or wrong of moral goodness. One can surrender, sacrifice, and even, as we hear frequently, kill the conscience. It can be regulated through adaptation to moral standards.

Proper feeding of the mind is significant. If clean, pure, and noble thoughts are fed into the mind, it will perform accordingly. If impure, dishonest thoughts are fed into the mind, it will perform accordingly. The mind, to a large extent, becomes what it feeds on. Good literature is good food for the mind whereas pornographic material is hurtful. As one would not eat poisonous food for the physical body, one should not allow poisonous food to be dumped into the mind. One cannot deal in impurities without coming into contact with some of the impurities.

Just as exercise is important to physical growth, exercise is important to mental growth. Both physical and mental exercise are important to mental health and growth. An idle brain might well be the devil's workshop. Idleness of the brain will give birth to a plethora of things: procrastination, indecision, unprepared-ness, and dullness. The brain will rust out quicker than it will wear out. One never gets too old to exercise the brain, and one never gets too old to learn something new. The unused mind is like an inkwell unused; it will eventually dry up. I believe that the more the mind is used the more it can be used.

There is no such thing as total neutrality or total inactivity of the mind. Even in sleep the mind is working. Experiments have been made proving that individuals can learn even during sleep. Reports tell of foreign languages having been played during sleeping hours, and it has been conclusively proven that those subjected learn the language played more easily and more quickly. But please don't try this in place of hard study when exams are approaching.

Dreams are another part of your mental activity. We do not know the cause of dreams nor the interpretation of them. Our dreams are scenarios, plays, and experiences in which we are both the author and the hero. They flash in and out of the sleeping mind like shadows.

There may be limitless activities possible if we could tap and use all possible levels of the mind including the unconscious and the subconscious as well as what is called ESP—extrasensory perception.

Imagination is a child and stimulus of the mind. It is a worthy tool to have in the building of a life. There is creativity in each one of us. The creative mind that thinks up ideas must not allow the judicial mind to negate their usefulness through criticizing them. Develop your imaginative powers.

There are three practical approaches to help you make remarkable use of your mind. Much of my time during my twenty-three years as president of Belmont College has been given to helping our students learn these approaches.

The first approach is to seek diligently to develop a strong, healthy mind. Your mind can be what you want it to be. If joggers push themselves so that they can run easily six to ten miles a day, and they do, then why shouldn't the mind be likewise pushed?

The adoption and the development of mental goals are essential in having a strong, healthy mind. The commitment to excellence is a worthwhile goal. Shoddy work should be taboo. Anything less than one's best is not good enough. The oft-quoted saying, "Hitch your wagon to a star, keep your seat, and there you are" is only half true. The first part is good, but keeping one's seat won't get you there. Too much lead in the middle part of one's body will overload the takeoff and prevent soaring.

The next thing that follows goal setting is the practice of self-discipline. You must make yourself do what is necessary to accomplish your goals. You are your own boss. Don't pass the buck or put the blame on someone else. Don't be a crybaby. You are in charge. In the practice of discipline, try to "spit and polish" your powers of concentration. Quietness aids concentration. Willpower will help you to focus your mental powers upon a given concern or matter. The power of concentration is like taking a magnifying glass and focusing the sun's rays through that glass upon a piece of paper. When that is done, the light and heat of the sun's rays are intensified and likely the paper will catch on fire. Quiet meditation is a viable part of concentration and will provide an atmosphere beneficent to concentration.

A strong, healthy mind grows out of continual use through study, much reading, and wholesome environment. A student once stated, "Professor, the average person reads only about one book a month."

"Oh, yes, I know, and that is why they are just average."

Make friends with good books. Select those books that have stood the test of the decades and the centuries, for a book is a new one until you have read it. This calls to mind another episode involving the dean-student relationship. A student commented to the academic dean, "Dean, is it correct that this college has only 100,000 volumes in the library?"

Quickly the dean replied, "That is correct. But when you have read all of those, we will then have a few more for you."

There is another approach to take in developing a strong, healthy mind which is not as obvious but is, nonetheless, useful and available. Try to tap the unconscious for assistance every now and then. It is there waiting to be called upon. It has been suggested that tapping the unconscious calls for three stages of activity. First, when a matter is under consideration, investigate fully and carefully every facet connected with it. Then, second, put those facts and findings into a phase called incubation. Leave them alone for a while and then go back and the third stage, illumination, will appear. Experience has taught me that the sequence works.

One of the most potent factors in developing a strong, healthy mind is religious faith. The apostle Paul, in writing to his son in the ministry said, "God hath not given us the spirit of fear; but of power, and of love, and of a sound mind" (2 Tim. 1:7). A poem on the wall in Chester Cathedral, England, expands on Paul's statement in our everyday language and is very suggestive:

> Give me a good digestion, Lord,
>   And also something to digest;
> Give me a healthy body, Lord,
>   And sense to keep it at its best;

Give me a healthy mind, O Lord,
   To keep the good and pure in sight,
Which, seeing sin, is not appalled,
   But finds a way to set it right.
Give me a mind that is not bored,
   That does not whimper, whine or sigh;
Don't let me worry overmuch
   About the fussy thing called "I";
Give me a sense of humor, Lord,
   Give me the grace to see a joke,
To get some happiness in life
And pass it on to other folk.[3]

Strong religious faith, rooted and grounded in our Judeo-Christian heritage, is a good antidote for worry, fear, hatred, envy, and jealousy—all the enemies of a healthy mind.

A second good approach in mental development is to *catch the intellectual itch*. It should be at least a six-year itch covering the years sixteen through twenty-two, but it will easily become the seven-year itch when covering fully both the sixteenth and twenty-second years. It is a profitable itch when attacking the mind, will, and emotions. It produces rather than a painful sensation a pleasant desire and feeling.

Such an itch can be caught if you associate with those who have the itch. The intellectual itch is both caught and taught. It is contagious and transferable. I can name some people who have had the intellectual itch and though being dead can still give you and others the itch. Read a biography of Albert Schweitzer, Albert Einstein, or Thomas Jefferson, and you are sure to catch it.

If you want the itch, it comes by finding those things that are itch prone. Use your imagination. Be curious. Inquire into the nature of things. Study the origin of things, the starry sky, the minuteness of the atom, the complexities of the computer, other marvels of science, and you will succumb to the itch fever. Some people never get the fever because they think they understand everything already.

Stay alert because, in seizing opportunities of self-renewal and self-development, you will no doubt breathe the itch spirit.

History tells us about one of the greatest of all the Greeks who ever lived—the great Hellene, Alexander the Great, who on parting from his tutor, Aristotle, heard him say, "Alexander, never forget the difference between the Greek and the barbarian."

Alexander replied, "Sir, I will make the world Greek. There will be no Greeks and barbarians, just Greeks." The pupil caught the itch from the tutor and conquered the then known world while at the same time spreading Hellenistic culture.

An intellectual itch should be properly doctored and cared for. It is wise to scratch and scratch the intellectual itch, for one cannot get an omelet without breaking the egg. Just as most people pay a doctor for advice and take the prescription to the drugstore for filling by the druggist, some people never take the doctor's advice, nor do they take the doctor's prescription as directed. Maybe it is not trite to say that if you are to scratch out a successful living you must scratch your intellectual itch every inch, for "life is hard by the yard, but by the inch it is a cinch if you scratch every inch of the way."

A third way to develop a strong, healthy mind is to have a mind at peace. If the mind finds itself warring with its emotions, will, and convictions, there is no peace. A happy mind is a healthy mind. A peaceful mind is a strong mind.

Ideally, most of us are looking for financial security and inner peace and happiness. Financial security, in the midst of our uncertain economic climate, is difficult to obtain. Inner peace of mind and happiness are about as difficult to possess.

There are some things that can be done to help bring about peace of mind. Tranquilizers and other drugs are not the answer. Alcohol is not the answer. Try to practice the art of maintaining equanimity. While a student doing my doctoral work, a friend of mine across the hall was counting loudly to ten. I asked, "Wally, why are you counting?"

His hasty reply was this, "Well, you can see I just knocked my desk light to the floor, and it broke. I am counting to ten to allow my anger to subside." Another good practice is to have what it is reported that President Harry Truman had: "A foxhole in my mind." It was a place of security and quietness.

Peace of mind that brings about a strong, healthy mind can be achieved by exerting all the faith you can muster, by placing all of your faith in that hope which springs eternal in the human breast, and by giving all your love.

Faith says that behind the clouds the sun is still shining. Faith infers that God's tomorrow will be better than today. Faith gives one something to stabilize oneself in the midst of a storm. A dear old man was asked how he maintained his equanimity during the severest of storms. He shared this formula, "Well, you see, I read in the Bible that it came to pass, never that it came to stay." What faith! I urge you to have faith in faith.

Hope is a desired expectation. Hope gives one an enthusiastic, positive outlook on life. The psalmist, writing centuries ago, urged his readers to seek happiness through hope, "Happy is he that hath the God of Jacob for his help, whose hope is in the Lord his God" (Ps. 146:5). "But I will hope continually, and will yet praise thee more and more" (Ps. 71:14). The prophet Joel proclaimed, "The Lord will be the hope of his people, and the strength of the children of Israel" (Joel 3:16). Hope that is founded in God is a source of real mental strength. I urge you to have hope against hope.

Love can be the alkali to neutralize the acids of hate, fear, jealousy, and anxiety.

Love is an anointing oil, a balm in Gilead. Love is the greatest thing in the world, for God is love. Practice love always and in all ways.

A strong, healthy mind can be yours. Your mind is your kingdom. Rule it well. Try to keep all your subjects happy. May cleanliness and charity be practiced and shared. You are endowed with a remarkable mind, one that will help you in meeting the challenge.

Notes

1. Ardis Whitman, *A New Image of Man* (New York: Appleton-Century-Crofts, Inc.), pp. 15-16.
2. Milton, *Paradise Lost*, I 254.
3. As found in Charles T. Holman, *The Religion of a Healthy Mind* (New York: Round Table Press, Inc., 1939).

3

You Are a Precious Soul

You and I are not worth much materially. Our bodies won't last much more than threescore and ten years. We are precious souls destined for eternity. Every person is both body and soul. There is a physical and spiritual nature residing in each one of us.

Cicero was right when he said, "Whatever that be which thinks, which understands, which wills, which acts, it is something celestial and divine, and on that account must necessarily be eternal." In other words there is a God-given blank in us. You are *precious to God* and responsible to him for your precious soul. The Bible says that, though one were to gain the whole world and lose his soul, he would profit nothing thereby (Mark 8:36). That is a startling contrast. It indicates the preciousness and value of the soul, that place where you can meet God or choose to exclude God.

The soul is that part of a person most closely akin to God. When man was created in the image of God he became a living soul (Gen. 2:7), and took on some Godlike attributes. It would be false of me to infer that humans possess those distinctive divine traits of God: omnipotence, omniscience, and omnipresence. Humans never have been and never will be all-powerful. They do not, regardless of their great intellectual achievements, possess all knowledge, for they have far more to learn than that which they have learned. Regardless of the travel capabilities we possess, we cannot be everywhere at the same time. Humanity's kinship with God is on different levels.

One of our constant weaknesses is the attempt to make God in our image and ascribe to him human traits. We want to think of

God as walking and talking, eating and sleeping, working and resting, but these are human, not divine, traits.

You Are an Image of God

I don't want to get into theological water over our heads, but it is important that we take a look at eight attributes which we possess that are akin to God and substantiate the fact that we are fashioned in God's image.

God possesses all knowledge, and we possess an intellectual nature which yearns for knowledge and struggles to acquire knowledge. God is also the source of all knowledge.

God has a rational nature. He thinks straight. Humans are rational beings with the capacity to reason, judge, and draw conclusions.

God is a righteous God who hates evil. He is bent on evil's destruction. Human beings are possessed of a moral nature which helps them sort out good and evil. Because of our moral nature, we too should be bent on evil's destruction.

God is a God of love, and he yearns for the fellowship of his creation. People, too, are emotional beings with the capacity for feeling. We can love or hate.

Human beings are endowed with a will, that power of controlling one's actions. God has perfect willpower, and everything he does is in accordance with that will.

God, who has absolute freedom, gave people the power of choice so as not to make them mere puppets in his hands. Human beings can choose good or evil, obedience or disobedience, God or mammon.

God is the ruler of the world. He can measure the waters in the hollow of his hand and measure the heavens with the span of his hand. He can place the dust of the earth in a measure, weigh the mountains in scales, and the hills in a balance (Isa. 40:12). The earth is God's, and the heavens speak of his glory. In creating human beings in his image, God made people to have dominion over the lower orders of creation.

God is eternal, and people long for eternal life. Augustine

once said, "We are restless, O God, until we rest in thee." People feel within their souls that God has for weary feet the gift of eternal rest.

Pay Attention to Your Soul Murmurs

It would be totally unreal to treat anything as precious as the human soul in a careless, indifferent manner. Yet so many young people today have what we might call "soul murmurs" and pay no attention to the cause of the murmurs. When one speaks of a heart murmur, the reference may be to a serious congenital condition. So it is with a soul murmur; do not take it lightly. Since the soul is the key part of human spiritual nature and resides in the body, it is important that the desires of the flesh not overcome the things of the spirit.

Many, many times the soul has been severely affected by the excessives of the flesh—soul murmurs. The emotional passion of pleasure and feeling has found expression and satisfaction in the philosophy of far too many young people of "eating, drinking, and making merry." It is the old Epicurean idea of sensual gratification and luxurious tastes. It is highly deceitful and deceitfully damaging to both body and soul.

Not long ago my wife and I attended a professional baseball game. Just in front of us were two young couples. I would have guessed their ages to be between eighteen and twenty-two years. They held in their hands cups of beer. They looked like fine, wholesome young people. Throughout the game they spent their time getting other cups of beer and going to the rest rooms. I doubt if they knew the score of the game at any time. Their whole attention was devoted to seeing how much beer they could down. Such action can be the beginning of a very dangerous habit. It is certain that dignity and self-respect cannot be preserved by alcohol. There is a spiritual law which can be translated something like this: don't turn your nose up at God and think you can get by with it, for what you sow you reap (see Gal. 6:7).

Material things to satisfy physical desires cause a soul murmur. People are more than things. Things are habit forming. Have you ever stopped to think how many different gadgets and mechanical things we use to get going in the morning, such as alarm clock, toaster, hair dryer, coffee pot, razor, and tooth-brush. We are a civilization of things, increasingly subjected to high pressure advertisement to buy even more. No one has yet to step forward and claim that more things possessed causes higher happiness or greater spirituality. The contrary is true. The more one has the more one wants. The possession of things seems to produce the want of more things. Dr. Billy Graham said on television recently that he had never seen a moving truck following a hearse.

Today, probably more than at any other time, people are striving for money and security. The Golden Rule has been redefined as the "rule of gold." He who has the gold makes the rules. Money is a god. The lack of it or the desire for it has engrossed our minds, gripped our actions. We are a civilization that has been termed "money mad." We struggle for it, surrender our convictions to get it, and waste our lives spending it for things that have little or no value. There are as many failures among the people who have made money as among the people with few of life's possessions. Money is bad insurance for health and happiness, especially when the thought of money obsesses a person. It can easily affect rational powers, will, intellect, and emotions.

In 1923, ten of the world's great financiers met at the Edgewater Beach Hotel. They seemed to be on top of the world. They had plenty of money. Life for them seemed to roll on and on. Twenty-five years later this is what had happened to some of them:

Charles Schwab, president of a large steel company, lived for five years on borrowed money and died in bankruptcy.

Samuel Insull, president of one of the greatest utilities, became a penniless fugitive from justice.

Howard Hopson, president of the largest gas company, was insane when he died.

Arthur Cotton, considered the greatest wheat speculator, died abroad, insolvent.

Richard Whitney, president of the New York Stock Exchange, spent time in Sing Sing Prison.

Albert Fall, member of the president's cabinet, was pardoned from prison so he could die at home.

The bear of Wall Street, Jesse Livermore, died a suicide.

Money is a good servant, but a very poor master.

Daily Exercises for the Soul

There are several positive exercises that, when done, will affect the soul significantly and cause fruit to be produced. First, because the body and the soul are in close relationship, the health of one is essential to the health of the other. A good, clean body is necessary for the enrichment of the soul. Our bodies are the temples of God, and his Spirit indwells Christians. God should never be asked to inhabit a dirty body. I have noticed how careful many young people are with their first car. They wash, clean, polish, and take unusual care of it. The slightest thing wrong with the car gets immediate and personal attention. It is their pride and joy. Is not the body more important than a car? Should it not be given careful and thoughtful care? Dirty thoughts, impure actions, and careless use of the body are distasteful to God and detrimental to the soul's health. A car wouldn't last very long if it got the kind of treatment some young people give their bodies.

Second, the mind should be fashioned according to those things that are wholesome, pure, and Christlike. One cannot dump "garbage thoughts" into the mind and expect pure, white second thoughts. The mind should be respected and served with high and noble thoughts. A dirty thought stains the mind like black ink stains a white handkerchief. There can be no healthy soul when it has to associate with a dirty mind. Even though initially the mind of a young person may tend to reject impure thoughts and off-color jokes and remarks, sooner or later resistance breaks down and there is a craving for more filth and dirt.

Every individual needs several guards posted at vantage points: one at the mouth to control what goes into the stomach, one at the gate of one's mind to see what goes in and out of the mind, one upon each ear lobe to filter what goes through the ear gate, and one at the pupil of each eye to control the traffic through the doors of the eyes because whatever goes through the ears and the eyes goes also into the mind.

Third, it is highly important that you walk uprightly, circumspectly. Persons are the only creatures created by God to walk upright. So you are gifted with a physical body that, even by design and operation, is meant to point you toward the Creator. Our walk, our habits, and our desires are an outgrowth of the cultivation and consent of the mind and soul. It is highly prudent that all young persons watch where they are going, where they intend to go, and where the crowd they are with is going. If the direction of the crowd is contrary to your wishes and commitments, then try to change the direction of the crowd; but if that is not possible, then it is time to change crowds. I have seen many fine, upright young people led astray by following the wrong crowd, by succumbing to the bright lights and peer pressures. Don't give in; don't give way but give leadership; give a clarion call to spiritual matters.

Fourth, for the soul to grow as the body grows, the soul must be fed "soul food." There is a verse in Paul's letter to his friends in Philippi which almost comprises a grocery list of food to be used for the soul. "Finally, brothers, whatever is true, whatever is worthy of reverence, whatever is just, whatever is pure, whatever is lovely, whatever is of good repute, if virtue is anything, if honor is anything, be always thinking about these" (Phil. 4:8, Centenary). What a smorgasbord for the soul. If you like good food, try these Spirit-filled foods.

Soul Fruit

When proper care and attention are given to the spirit, then there is an abundant harvest of spiritual fruit. Love, joy, peace, long-suffering, gentleness, goodness, faith, meekness, and temperance are all fruit of the Spirit (Gal. 5:22-23).

It is very hard to be patient when our patience is tried by another's folly and false accusations. Did you ever do anything through impatience, such as severely criticize your friend when you should have waited and found out more of the actual situation? Patience is hard to master.

It is hard to be gentle and meek when you have the urge to strike back when falsely maligned or attacked by another. Don't yield to the urge to give another person a piece of your mind because pieces are usually sharp and detached from the real core and because too many broken off pieces of the mind shatter one's perception and rational powers. Did you ever bite your tongue to keep from becoming boisterous and vindictive? Have you ever heard your name used in derogatory terms? It would have been easy to fire back with verbal darts. But gentleness and meekness are attributes, not of weakness but of strength. To be gentle is to be refined in manners. To be meek is to be tolerant and understanding.

Goodness is good, but not good enough. Be good for something, not just for goodness' sake. Let goodness rise from the ashes of purity, honesty, and justice.

Temperance is a hard virtue to acquire. We all like to eat. We probably eat too much. This is intemperance. Extra weight is hard to carry. It taxes the heart. It dulls the mind. It slackens the pace. We all like to watch television programs, but too much of anything is too much. Time is wasted, nothing much is gained, opportunities are lost, and work goes undone.

I have never in all my life met a person who started drinking alcoholic beverages who intended to become an alcoholic. I have worked with many—spent hours with them. The story is always the same. "I started to drink with the crowd." "I took a dare." "I thought I had to drink to be sociable." "It was the thing everyone was doing." "I let it get too strong a hold of me." "I couldn't say no." If one never starts a bad habit, one will never have to break a bad habit. Everything begun by an individual has some impact on that individual's life. Watch carefully for the end of the tunnel.

Where will this bring me out, into the sunshine or into the dark clouds of alcoholism? A good motto for every young person is: "Be wise, don't alcoholize."

What I have tried to point out is that the habits and conduct of the body affect the growth and health of the soul. Both operate in close association with each other. Form good physical habits. Practice good things for the soul. Leave nothing to chance. It will take body, mind, and soul to meet the challenge.

4

You Are a
Vital Part of Society

The society in which you live has room for moving around. There is plenty of room for growth. You really can become an important part of society if you set your sights in that direction. I don't mean that in your high school or college environment you should strut as an egotistical bird. I don't think the world outside wants that kind of person.

Any person wrapped up in himself makes a mighty small package and in most cases is unwanted. Most of us have seen such a proud, selfish person who prays, "O, God, bless me and Mary, John and Sara, us four and no more." He is the kind who would be so heavenly as to be of no earthly value.

We are needed more on earth than we are needed in heaven. The heavenly society has no hunger, no war, no crime, no disease, no cutthroat competition. But not so with earthly society. That society needs persons who are big—big in heart, big in service, big in self-giving. If you want to become that sort of person, I can offer some rather solid comments.

You Own Many Shares of Society's Stock

You have inherited many shares of society's stock. Additionally, you have earned a few more. There is no way you can accurately estimate the number of shares coming to you through the channel of history. The achievements of many, the knowledge and wisdom of others, and the philanthropic contributions of some who have made possible wonderful libraries, outstanding museums, great art masterpieces, and scientific discoveries place great value upon the shares you have inherited.

There are many cultural traditions which have enriched our society. You have inherited those shares also. We live in a society that has an appreciation of an individual's rights and freedom. We believe that all people are born free and equal. We have an economic climate in which the free enterprise system offers everyone a chance to ply her trade and test her skills. We are not fenced in by laws that destroy our initiative.

We have inherited many shares of stock in the world's finest educational system that is free for all through the high school level. Education is no longer for the privileged few. It opens its door to all regardless of race, creed, or religion. There is ample opportunity for personal growth and development. There are free lunches and free textbooks for the needy. What a system!

Think of our religious inheritance. It, too, is most unusual. We have churches in which we may worship freely. In our country religion is respected, protected, and even rejected if one so desires. There is no coercion by the government. The spirit and tenets of our Judeo-Christian faith are interwoven into the warp and woof of the fabric of our society, making it a wholesome and compatible place in which to live and rear children. Your inheritance is great.

But You Are Heavily in Debt

Even though you inherited much of the stock you own, there is still a price you must pay to possess it.

Today you may drive on miles of good roads and streets. Neither you nor I paid the cost of those streets or roads. We could not. The cost has been borne by many. We may have paid some of the cost through taxes, but we enjoy what others have helped to pay. Country roads were scenic but dangerous in winter time. Mud, deep ruts, and ditches made transportation hazardous and unpleasant. I recall, while a high school lad, helping to push cars out of the mud. I have been splattered by the mud thrown from the spinning wheels. I have had to clean many a pair of muddy shoes. My mother has gotten after me for tracking dirt into the house that I carried in from muddy roads.

The good streets and sidewalks are ours to enjoy and use. We did not lay or pay for either. We owe many a heavy debt of gratitude.

The services rendered by our city government are beyond our personal means. We could not *individually* afford to maintain police protection, fire protection, or waste removal. All of these services come to us through *collective support* which means we are heavily in debt to each other. We owe something in return to our city. You and I are a vital part of the thing we call "our city." The debt hangs constantly over our heads.

Our municipal parks, public libraries, and civic halls are constant reminders of the debt we owe to our city and society.

The miracles of modern medicine shared with us through our public health services add another debt to the growing list. We no longer fear the dreaded diseases of typhoid, tuberculosis, or spinal meningitis. Plagues that once wiped out a community or family are no longer lurking in the shadows. Generally, we are a very healthy society. There are diseases that we inflict upon ourselves through undue stress and strain and that we communicate to others through impure and sensual living, such as venereal diseases. Many killer diseases have been brought under control through available vaccinations, immunity shots, and strong antibiotics. These strides in medicine and health care have not happened automatically but have come after long and arduous research.

The various ethnic groups that populate our nation have made lasting contributions to our society. And so the debt goes on and on. Blacks have made marvelous contributions to American music. They have given to the world an example of personal faith in a living Lord. The Indians who were pushed aside unfairly as our pioneers pushed onward have kept us conscious of our lovely land and the beautiful things of nature. People from other countries have settled here and are leaving a positive imprint. The Scots have impressed upon us the value of frugality and careful use of our possessions. The Dutch have given us a sense of industry and careful use of our resources, and the list could go on. The various religious groups have made their contributions to our society in significant ways. Roman Catholics have shown us the meaning of religious fraternity, religious education of constituents, and a respect and loyalty to the clergy as men of God. The Jews have kept their faith in one God very much alive and have placed great emphasis upon the moral precepts of the Old Testament laws. They have practiced family loyalty. Protestants, including Baptists, have permeated our society with a strong evangelistic spirit, a devotion to missions to the ends of the earth, and the worth and freedom of the individual in the context of the priesthood of believers.

The geographical divisions of our land have made unique and specific contributions to our society. The people of the West have been adventurers, possessed of a free spirit. Those of the North have been hardy souls, strongly committed to our national development. Those of the East have pioneered in educational opportunities and commerce. The South has given to society a spirit of hospitality and concern for each other.

I ask now a very simple question: Can you and I ever pay our debt to society? We can try, and we will try in service rendered.

You Have a Growing Shadow

Robert Louis Stevenson wrote the poem "My Shadow":

> I have a little shadow that goes in and out with me,
> And what can be the use of him is more than I can see.
> He is very, very like me from the heels up to the head;
> And I see him jump before me, when I jump into my bed.
>
> The funniest thing about him is the way he likes to grow—
> Not at all like proper children, which is always very slow;
> For he sometimes shoots up taller like an India-rubber ball,
> And he sometimes gets so little there is none of him at all.
>
> He hasn't got a notion of how children ought to play,
> And can only make a fool of me in every sort of way.
> He stays so close beside me, he's a coward you can see;
> I'd think shame to stick to nursie as that shadow sticks to me!
>
> One morning, very early, before the sun was up,
> I rose and found the shining dew on every buttercup;

But my lazy little shadow, like an errant sleepy-head,
Had stayed at home behind me and was fast asleep in bed.

The shadow I want to look at is that of influence. Every person in society influences other persons and is in return influenced by others. It is not possible to run away from life. You cannot get off of this whirling globe. Your influence on others can be good or bad. Your life in society can cast either a shadow that will make society stronger and more wholesome, or it can cast a shadow that will darken and damage the spirit and fellowship of the neighborhood and society.

Careless words can damage and hurt one another. Have you ever been stung by another's tart and terse reply? Have others been stung by your remarks? Walking among friends leaves a shadow of influence like a cloud passing in front of the rays of the sun.

Here is an exercise you might find helpful. Think of yourself walking down the corridor of one of your classroom buildings. The hallway is filled with friends and classmates. As they see you, what do they think? What do they feel? Are their thoughts pure and uplifting, or do they recall something—some remark or some little deed—that places you in a different category? Your shadow is certainly in evidence. As you walk down the corridor, your influence, large or small, is there.

Influence is like good perfume: it can be detected as you walk just as perfume is smelled as you come within its range.

There is no way to use cosmetics to improve the looks of a shadow, but there are ways to affect the contour and appearance of your shadow of influence. Let each day be counted as a day when some worthy action is done. Let each opportunity be bought up in service and love for others. Get in the habit of thinking about your shadow. Think about it as you go in and out among your fellow students. Think about it when you find yourself on a date. Think about it when you find yourself in a huddle with your friends. Think about it now. Think about it later on today.

Your Fraternities and Sororities Are Calling on You

There are several fraternities and sororities in need of your help. I am not thinking about social, Greek-letter societies. I am thinking about four special groups that are a part of the society in which you reside.

The first group of people to consider is a large group whom you may never see or meet. This group is very crucial to you and your life. Their actions, thoughts, and desires readily become a part of your life. They can create riots, revolutions, or crusades that quickly determine the tempo of your environment. They can scatter ill winds of bigotry, hate, and false accusations which blow quickly into your atmosphere of activity. In turn, you, unknown to them, can have similar effects upon their lives. Just as a scorching ill wind can blow north or south, east or west, so can a cool, soothing wind of love, concern, and brotherhood blow in all directions.

Second, there are those people whom you may associate with occasionally or just one time. They influence you; you influence them. They need you; you need them. You are somewhat closer to this group than the former group. Can you recall persons whom you met only one time, yet your memory of that meeting is still fresh and vivid in your mind? Why is this true? Why did they impress you? Was it what they said? Was it the manner in which they said it? Was it their look or personality? Was it their status or rank in their profession? Who is the most impressive person you ever met? Why did you pick that person? On the other hand, did you impress that person? If not, why not; if so, why? Once I saw Winston Churchill in Jamaica. I shall never forget that occasion. I stood at the airport in Kingston pushing and shoving to get a glimpse of him. He strode through the terminal with confidence. His eyes were penetrating. His presence indicated that here was a man of destiny. I met him later through his writings and found that my initial impressions were right. He has influenced my life.

Third, there are those who make up your student body and

your social group. These are people you live with, study with, and celebrate with. Some are your favorites. You know their likes and dislikes. You eat with them, share with them in confidence. They make a great difference in your life. In this inner circle of friends, you find a oneness of spirit and desire. This group can be very powerful in shaping the thoughts and actions of its members. Peer pressure is a strong force within the group. Here is where paradoxes exist. You often feel that you know the group so well that you need not give attention to your thoughts and actions. The opposite, however, is true because no group can function maximally or efficiently unless constant attention is paid to it by each member. You may think you know a special person so well that there is never any need of trying to learn that person better. In your complete devotion to that one, you may overlook obvious weaknesses or opportunities. Give much attention to your membership in this group.

The fourth group is your family and relatives. They know you best. They love you best. They know your faults and your virtues. They have placed their faith in you. In many cases, they have sacrificed for you. When I left home at the age of sixteen in 1930 to enter college, my parents were unable to provide financial support for my college expenses. I was on my own, yet I was not on my own. My mother wrote me weekly. Frequently she enclosed a few postage stamps or occasionally a dollar or two. Those were the height of the Depression years. I knew that my mother had gotten the money to pay for the stamps or the money to enclose in the letter from the sale of butter, eggs, or chickens. My father found it difficult to make enough money to pay the interest to the bank on the money he had borrowed to buy his small farm. He would have gladly shared, but he had little to share. Their sacrifices were real. I have never forgotten their love and support; though meager financially, it was great in love and concerned care. I couldn't have made it without them. My sisters were equally supportive. I was fortunate. I imagine in the same respect you are also fortunate. I am different today because of their help and encouragement yesterday. That small fraternity known as family is calling and will continue to call upon us through their expectancy of our devotion and achievements. We bear their names. Let us make them proud.

You Can Really Be "Big" if You Play by the Higher Rules

You can make a great difference in society. You can make a tremendous impact on your campus. You can play an important role. You need to be involved. You must be a participator, not a commentator. Many times at baseball games I have become very amused listening to the big and the little, young and old, trying to tell the pitcher how to pitch the ball or trying to tell the batter how and where to hit the ball. I know that none of those giving such free advice could either pitch or hit. Their advice is hollow. First, then, make up your mind that you aren't going to criticize the spirit on your campus or the conditions of society until you try to do something to improve the spirit on campus or those societal conditions.

It would be unwise for you to gauge your conduct and involvement by those who do things only for personal, selfish gain. They are striving to become important in another way, a false way. Always treat your contemporaries as persons, not as things. Remember that they too have thoughts, feelings, and plans. I have said many times that there are basically two kinds of students on most campuses: the problem creator and the problem solver. Into which group do you fall?

There are some fundamental rules by which the game of life should be played in society. It is not possible for each person to make the rules. You can readily see that such a plan would not work in the early morning traffic, for there would be nothing but chaos at every street intersection. Class schedules cannot be determined by allowing students to come and go when they desire. Rules are to assist in regulating, coordinating, and directing, not to regiment.

Among the many rules and right practices by which the game of life is played, three are of major concern. First, there is the rule articulated by Immanuel Kant, a German philosopher of the eighteenth century, who wrote in 1788 in his *Critique of Practical Reason*: "Two things fill the mind with ever new and increasing admiration and awe, the oftener and the more steadily we reflect on them: the starry heavens above and the moral law within." According to Kant, the moral law within should produce an oughtness in each one, which he called "a categorical imperative." That oughtness should cause each person to treat every other person as a person, not as a thing. This means that we are not to maneuver others for our advantage. We are not to treat them conditionally, but absolutely as persons and not as stepping-stones for personal gain to be discarded when no longer needed. The basic principle here is that of the supreme value of the individual personality.

Several months ago we had a family in our home for dinner. After dinner we sat enjoying each other in conversation. Our guests were comprised of a husband and wife and their two children, a young man and young woman. The young man of high school age said that they were permitted to drink soft drinks in the classroom. His mother questioned that statement to which he replied, "Oh, Mom, I drank part of Jim's cola."

She quickly retorted, "Oh, Son, you didn't drink from the same bottle did you?"

"Yes, Mother, he is a Baptist, and he doesn't have germs." Touché! Baptists are not automatically virtuous or first-class citizens while all others are second-class. To give other persons a second-class rating is to be hypercritical and insincere. This is dangerous action for a campus or a culture or a religion.

William James, an American philosopher and psychologist of the nineteenth and early twentieth centuries, propounded another good rule in his *Essays on Faith and Morals, The Moral Equivalent of War* when he wrote: "A permanent successful peace-economy cannot be a simple pleasure economy. . . . We must make new energies and hardihoods continue the manliness to which the military mind so faithfully clings. Martial virtues must be the enduring cement; intrepidity, contempt of softness, surrender of private interest, obedience to command, must still remain the rock upon which the states are built. . . . It is only a question of blowing on the spark till the whole population gets incandescent, and on the ruins of the old morals of military honor, a stable system of morals and civic honors builds itself up."

This we have called the "moral imperative" which places a strong commitment and support of those virtues and character traits which produce strong persons who are willing to endure hardships and censorship in order to purge the evil and preserve the good in society. Purity, honesty, justice, equality, and brotherhood are among those moral laws.

There is a third rule which I choose to call the "Christian imperative" which has its rootage in the tenets of our biblical faith. The Ten Commandments of the Old Testament spoke of four "thou shalt nots" with reference to God and man and six "thou shalt nots" with reference to man and man. You will find these in Exodus 20.

Christ came and took the negative aspects of the law and gave them a positive frame of reference. He made it very clear that the same laws that govern his kingdom should govern society. Greatness in his kingdom is on the basis of service: "He that is greatest among you shall be your servant" (Matt. 23:11). That same principle applies in society: service above self. Caring, loving, and sharing are the watermarks of service. When our three daughters were growing up, we discovered that one of them no longer had her box of crayons. Upon being questioned by her mother, she replied, "Well, Mother, Catherine wanted some of them, so I ate them to keep her from having any." Before we could reason with her, we had to retrieve the colors from her stomach. I have thought of that little experience many, many times. Students and grownups act like that. Time and time again many of them seem to be doing things that say, "I'll indulge and gorge while I can. I don't want to lose this or share it with others. They can root for themselves. I'm all for myself."

Without trying to take away from the Ten Commandments or the marvelous Sermon on the Mount (Matt. 5—7), I would like to summarize the major teachings of the New Testament by listing what I have chosen to call "Thirteen Rules for Right Living on Campus or in Society."

"Thou shalt love the Lord thy God with all thy heart, and with all thy soul, and with all thy mind, and with all thy strength" (Mark 12:30).

"Thou shalt love thy neighbour as thyself" (Mark 12:31).

"Love your enemies" (Matt. 5:44).

"Seek ye first the kingdom of God, and his righteousness" (Matt. 6:33).

"Whosoever shall compel thee to go a mile, go with him twain" (Matt. 5:41).

"Whosoever shall smite thee on thy right cheek, turn to him the other also" (Matt. 5:39).

"Give to him that asketh thee," food, water or clothes (Matt 5:42; Matt. 25:35-36).

"All things whatsoever ye would that men should do to you, do ye even so to them" (Matt. 7:12).

"Bear ye one another's burdens" (Gal. 6:2).

"See then that ye walk circumspectly, . . . Redeeming the time" (Eph. 5:15-16).

"Let your speech be alway with grace, seasoned with salt, that ye may know how ye ought to answer every man" (Col. 4:6).

"Study to shew thyself approved unto God, a workman that needeth not to be ashamed, rightly dividing the word of truth" (2 Tim. 2:15).

"Upon the first day of the week let every one of you lay by him in store, as God hath prospered him" (1 Cor. 16:2).

The rules are there. The rules are clear. Play by the rules. You can really become a positive influence in society and on your campus. You can be somebody. You can help somebody. You will influence somebody. Strive to make an impact on your campus.

Section II
What Am I Doing Here?

Once you have decided who you are, your next big question is to decide what you are doing here. These are the first two big questions to ponder and to think about while meeting the challenges.

You and I have the happy privilege of trying to find out why we are here, especially at this time. There is no nobler search or quest than that which takes a person kneeling on a question mark of doubt and lifts him to stand tall on an exclamation mark of affirmation.

Every life has a purpose, and it should be the goal of every person to lay hold of that purpose. Many seek to lay hold of life's purposes through varied activities. Some think that all one has to do is drift with the tide, and the tide will bring one into the promised land. But that doesn't work. There are those who always go in the direction with the wind at their backs rather than face the winds that sweep down from the elevated heights. An old man was asked how he managed to get along so well with everyone. He replied, "I just put my mind in neutral and go where I am pushed." There is no better way to destroy selfhood and self-reliance than to shift into neutral. In this mechanized age, some young people feel that they are here merely to run errands for the computer or the company. But that is far from the essence of life.

There are some who seek to find the answer to the question, Why am I here? by mounting their iron steeds and dashing off madly in every direction at the same time. They equate purpose with speed and the major thing with the minor things. In that

respect, they are like the children who were taken to the circus
by the maid. All day long the youngsters wanted to ride the
merry-go-round. At the close of a hot and boring day for the
maid, the children once again asked to ride the merry-go-round.
Standing there watching them dismount from their last ride of
the day, the maid exhaustingly exclaimed, "Now, let me ask you
children one thing—you get off where you get on, and you get
on where you get off; you have spent all your money—now
where have you been?" Going in circles covers little mileage.

While trying to lay hold of the purpose in life, many spend too
much time looking for bargain values that don't exist, yet the
looking is very time consuming.

You would be amazed at the number of persons who trust to
luck to fill their baskets. Luck is composed primarily of hard
work, vision, and integrity. Others seek to find a pot of gold in a
far-off country rather than at the end of the rainbow of a life in
which the three primary colors of red, yellow, and blue are
properly mixed: the red of religion, the yellow of knowledge,
and the blue of morality.

A man once found a fifty cent piece and spent the rest of his
life looking down as he walked. During his lifetime he found 79
cents, fifteen buttons, a few pins, and a knife; but he had also
acquired stooped shoulders, downcast eyes, and a slow gait.
Very few people have ever stumbled upon wealth or a noble
purpose in life.

If you would seek to find out why you are here along with
about 3.5 billion others who inhabit earth, let me offer you four
good ways to pursue your quest. Search for truth, seek out your
options, live life to the fullest and best, and use well your time.
Learn from Christopher Columbus who discovered America in
1492. It has been said about him that when he left Genoa, Italy,
he did not know where he was going; when he arrived he did not
know where he was, and when he got back home he could not
tell his friends where he had been. But one thing he could tell
them, and that one thing is as current today as the days when he

was sailing the ocean blue with men who grew mutinous, "Sail on, sail on, and on." In other words, don't abandon the ship. Follow the gleam. Don't lose faith in your vision. Be a "little Columbus" as you meet the challenge.

5

Searching for Truth— The Real Thing

Humans are curious, quizzical, and questioning individuals. We look for answers to questions. We are not satisfied with things as they are. We want to change things. The unknown challenges us. The impossible lures us on. We can't sit still; we can't stand still. We can't keep quiet. We must be heard from. We want to know the facts. We want to know how things work. We are anxious to know the real thing, the truth of the matter.

Through the centuries people have been asking scientific questions such as: is the world round or flat? Is there life on other planets? Where did we come from? Can the aging process be reversed? Theologically the questions have run the gamut of everything from: is God real? and is there just one God? to can God be known personally? Other questions raised are: is sin displeasing to God? Is there a judgment day coming? With regard to one's personal life, people have been asking: how can I tell right from wrong? Am I responsible to anyone for anything, or shall I look after only number one? When I die, shall I live again?

All of these questions are attempts to find an answer, to see what works and to filter out the false from the true.

That's the Truth

It is not always easy to identify truth. Truth is sometimes surrounded by false ideas and misconceptions and must be ferreted out. Francis Bacon noted years ago that there are three parts to truth: first, the inquiry or the search, the wooing of truth; second, the knowledge of truth which is the presence of it;

third, the belief in truth which provides the enjoyment of it.

In John 18:38, Pontius Pilate, procurator of Judea at the time of the trial and crucifixion of Jesus, asked Jesus, "What is truth?" Pilate never got the answer to his question because he was unwilling to face up to the facts about Jesus. People have asked that question thousands of times since, and some have searched for the answer and have found the facts.

If there were no more to this question of truth than to say, "The real is true," we wouldn't have much to ponder. It would be easy to say that spring has gone into summer, summer into fall, and fall into winter; but there is more. There is truth that is not visible or tangible but comes from search, inquiry built on certain propositions and suppositions. These must be verified, established. Laboratories have lived and grown on this kind of truth. There is experiential truth, truth that comes through experience when a person can say, "I know this. I have seen it with my eyes. I have felt it. I have been there."

There are some great, unchanging truths that have sprung from our knowledge of God and his Word, the Bible. God is the source of all truth. His Word is truth. The contents of the Bible are true and worthy of full acceptance. Some of those truths which have stood the test of the ages are: there is one God. God is the Creator and Sustainer of the world. God is righteous and holy, no respecter of persons. Christ is the Son of God, the Redeemer of humanity. We are to treat our neighbors as ourselves. There will be no popular vote on changing the constitution of the universe. God, and God alone, makes that determination. We are not responsible to God for the movements of the stars, the planets, and the heavenly bodies; but we are responsible to God for our own movements and deeds.

Truth is neither weak nor helpless. It is no invalid. It needs no coddling, no pampering, no pushing in a stroller. It can stand alone. It may be distasteful to some, bitter to others, especially when it interferes with our accustomed way of doing things. There have been many who did not like the Ten Commandments, but the Commandments will never be repealed. There are many who do not agree with the teachings of the Sermon on the Mount, but these teachings cannot be overthrown.

Scientists have done a pretty good job of establishing certain basic truths, such as, the world is round, the law of cause and effect, water and oil don't mix, the law of action and reaction, and the presence of atoms and viruses.

There are certain moral and ethical truths which are operable and understandable. Honesty is a good practice. Cheating in the classroom is self-defeating. Obedience of the law is good. Disobedience produces a bad harvest.

I want to share with you an experience I had one fall morning when I was about twelve years of age. That morning my father was planning to shuck a wagonload of corn in the lower field. He had graciously excused me from helping him. As he drove by the house enroute to the field, I was throwing a ball against the front of the house trying to see if it would bounce back beyond my capability of catching it. Seeing this, my father stopped the team of mules and told me that I should not do that. The front of the house was not for that purpose. Then, too, he added that I would grow careless and throw the ball through one of the large windows. I immediately informed him of my athletic skills and prowess. I further added that if I should break a window I would replace it with money from my total savings of $2.00.

Wanting to let me learn the truth of such a situation—that no one is perfect and that we all tend to get careless—he proceeded to the lower field. I continued to throw the ball against the house. I thought I was good. But he had no more than gotten into the field when a careless throw sent the ball smashing through the window. It seemed to me that he shucked that load of corn in record time. For soon I heard him coming from the field. I wanted to distract him as long as I could. I met him at the gate and opened it for him. He knew from the past that such an action was not a usual one for me. He suspected something and glanced toward the house. He saw the broken window. Getting down from the wagon, he walked over to a piece of shrubbery in the yard and cut a switch. He laid it on me. I learned fast. That was a lesson of truth. I tried, every time I worked in the front yard, to kill that piece of shrubbery, but I never succeeded.

There are truths that history has taught us. Some of the lessons of history are: whom the gods would destroy, they first make mad with power; it is darkest before the dawn; the bee stings the flower to fertilize it. We would be smarter if we could learn these truths and accept them, but it seems that each generation must learn for itself that which preceding generations have learned. We don't come into the world endowed with wisdom. We must learn for ourselves. Parents can inform us, teachers can instruct us, but still we must learn for ourselves.

In the process of growing up, we learn certain truths. Every high school and college student has learned that fire will burn, strong winds can destroy, water and food are essential to plant life and human life, and no one is totally free to do as he pleases. These and many more truths we learn quickly while other truths come slowly.

We are slow to learn the truths that hatred, envy, and jealousy are enemies to society. We want to spurn the law of sowing and reaping. We prefer not to be held accountable for corporate acts. We much prefer to blame those acts on society and think that we thereby bear no responsibility. But who are we kidding? The truth is that we are a part of society. Society can be dealt with only by dealing with individuals.

The same attitude is taken toward the government, federal funds, and entitlement programs. Many citizens feel that the government is to blame for everything, that federal funds are limitless and self-generative, and that all entitlement programs entitle all who qualify for full and forever support. The truth is that the government is of the people, by the people, and for the people. Federal funds are out of your pocket and my pocket. We pay the taxes that provide those funds.

To Tell the Truth

I wish it were easy to always tell truth from error. That is not the case. It is not always easy to tell right from wrong. Harris

Franklin Rall, in his book *Christianity,* gives four tests of truth.[1] A consideration of these at this point will be most helpful. The four tests are:

1. The test of coherence. This is the test of consistency or agreement. We can check new ideas by this test. Does the idea fit in with the results of previous experience? There may be a necessity for modification of the old to fit in with the new, rather than to totally discard the new.

2. The test of inclusiveness. Here the fact or idea should take in all the fields of experience, bringing them into unity, not putting them at odds with each other.

3. The test of accessibility. Is this truth accessible to all and verifiable by all or is it simply a private opinion?

4. The test of verification by experience. Knowledge and truth come from life experiences, individual and racial, and should find further validation in additional experience.

As a student and in dealing with other students, you may be tempted at times to deviate from the truth. The temptations of cheating and lying are rather persistent ones. Cheating hits early in life, especially when unprepared for the test to be given or when it is expedient or easier to cheat than to study. The importance placed upon grades has caused many to cheat with the hope of improving their grades. Cheating has become a science, done so skillfully as to make detection almost impossible. Some have written information on sticks of chewing gum, copying the information, then chewing the gum to destroy the evidence. Others have been known to write facts on the cuffs of shirt sleeves, then turn the cuffs up to conceal the evidence. Some think to cheat in such fashion is smart. Regardless of how the cheating occurs or for whatever reason, cheating is wrong. It projects a moral weakness, destroying honesty and the sense of personal achievement. Cheating in school will lead to cheating in business, in family life, and in society. Grades gotten dishonestly are not worth having.

Lying is an easy trap to fall into when the truth seems to condemn us. For self-protection and self-justification, we quickly misstate a fact or misrepresent a condition. Somehow we think this manner of approach will shelter us from the consequences, but lying merely increases the problem. A chapel speaker told our students that he who lies must be able to invent twenty more lies to defend the first lie and that he who tells the truth does not need a good memory, for he needs no defense.

Some people lie for material gain, others lie to prevent personal embarrassment, while still others lie to deceive. In any form or fashion taken, lying is a weakness and a liability. It also plays into the hands of the devil and makes the liar one of his disciples. In God's sight, there are no white lies; they are all black.

I have in my possession a letter which I received years ago from one of our former student leaders. He had written to explain to me that the money which he had announced as being stolen from his car while serving in office was not actually stolen. He had used it for personal expense. His conscience was still bothering him. I was not totally surprised to receive the letter. I had felt that his explanation of the missing money was flimsy and untrue and that in time he would confess his error. In order to set the record straight, he stated in his letter to me that many people who were affected by his actions had been written, asking for forgiveness.

In this case, the lying of the young man had accomplished little, if anything. It had created mental torment for the liar and had caused him to face up to the truth. Facing up to the truth is sometimes hard, bitter, and painful. In fact, my friend said that "getting honest is one of the hardest things for me to do." But it was the mature thing for him to do. Repentance and confession have a good cathartic effect on those who will practice repentance and confession.

I am very glad to be able to indicate another chapter in the life of that young man. He is now a successful employee in a church in the South. He seems to be trying to make his life count on the side of truth and righteousness.

Think about the times you have handled the truth lightly:

perhaps cheated on an examination or lied about a matter of prime importance. Maybe you deceived your parents. How did you feel after the acts were committed? Did you feel good about yourself? In all honesty, did you not feel disappointed with yourself? Didn't you feel that you had destroyed a little pride and self-esteem? Did you not think of yourself as just something less than the best?

If there is something hankering within your soul that got there through some act of untruth or cheating, deal with it right now. Set the record straight. Make amends.

Several years ago I noticed on my bookshelf a book which I had borrowed from the seminary book store when I was the resident seminary manager for the Baptist Book Store of Louisville, Kentucky. In the seminary book store we sold new and used books. This was a used book, but I could not recall ever paying for it. After about twenty years out of the seminary, I wrote the manager of the downtown store, telling her that to the best of my recollection I had not paid for the book and, even though I did not purposely take it, I felt that I should share this with her and pay for the book. She was most gracious and understanding.

The beautiful thing about trying to make amends is that most people are forgiving and understanding. A tiny little scar might remain, but the recollection of such an act and such an effort to square things will serve a good purpose. Every time I see that book on my library shelf, I remember the facts connected with it. I am sure that the book has reminded me time and time again that books that I have not purchased or had given to me are not mine to possess.

It is a sad fact that many books are missing from library shelves and never come home, denying others the use of those books. To carry my personal experience one step further, I have just gotten up out of my chair at my typewriter table and gone into the adjacent room where most of my books are and pulled that book off the shelf and held it in my hand for a moment. It is different from all the other books I possess, some 2,500 in all. It came to me in a different way, and it speaks to me very clearly. You might be interested in the title of the book. It is entitled *Sin* and was written by T. DeWitt Talmage in 1901. Talmage was a great preacher of his day, a man whose speech was not a mere echo but a strong voice. Let me quote from that book, "Do not, because of seeming temporary advantage, give up your character. Under God that is the only thing you have to build on."[2]

Truth Is Stronger than Fiction

Truth has enduring power. It is not weak or emaciated. Bryant wrote some immortal words when he penned the following lines:

> Truth, crushed to earth shall rise again,—
> The eternal years of God are hers;
> But Error, wounded, writhes in pain,
> And dies amid his worshippers.[3]

Fiction, on the other hand, is temporary and without substance. Fiction is the art of fashioning, imaging, inventing something to serve one's purpose. It can be a figment of the imagination or a fabrication. It may taste good for a moment, but its sweetness may soon turn to sourness.

As a college president for twenty-three years, I had many experiences with students. One leaps to my mind just now. One bright morning a personality-plus type of youngster came into my office with a letter from his minister stating that due to religious convictions the young man should be excused from our required chapel services. I read the letter with intense interest, watching the young man all the while. He was very poker faced. I sensed something unusual about the letter but proceeded cautiously. I asked, even though there was a signature of the minister at the bottom of the letter, "Did your minister sign this?"

"Oh, yes sir, his signature is there, isn't it?" To which I replied in the affirmative but added, "Well, let me keep the letter. I know your minister quite well, and I will get in touch with him and explain the chapel services required of our students." He agreed to let me do that and left with instructions to return two days later.

Upon his return, I had to share with him the truth that his minister had said that he did not write the letter and that, furthermore, he thought it would be good for the young man to attend chapel. I had explained to the minister that even though we were a Baptist college we did not practice proselyting, nor did we attempt denominational indoctrination in our chapel services.

The young man seemed very disturbed to hear me say that I had talked with his minister. I felt the time had come for me to press for the truth and peel off the fiction.

Removing my watch from my arm and placing it on the desk, in plain view of the student, I said, "Friend, you have five minutes to tell me the truth about this deal. Remember, truth is spoken in my office, and I do not expect untruths to seek to find a place here."

The young man squirmed, shifted his feet, and looked down at the floor. Then, with a dejected look, he said, "The minister did not write or sign that letter. I got the yardman at the church to do it for me." I looked him straight in the eyes and saw disappointment, hurt, and sorrow. His trembling words came forth, "Well, I have made a fool of myself. I won't be able to look you in the eye when I see you on campus. What are you going to do with me?"

Sensing genuine remorse and regret, I told him to raise his head. "Listen, my friend, I am requesting that you do two things. First, go immediately to your minister and confess to him what you have tried to do, then have him call me stating that you have been there. After that, come back to my office." The young man left with haste and within two hours was back in my office. (His minister had called in the meantime.) I took him by the hand and said, "Look, you tried to get by with something, and you failed. This whole thing is between the two of us. I am not going to do anything else other than to tell you to let this be one of life's grandest lessons about truth. When you see me on the campus, look up, look me right in the eye, and give me a friendly greeting."

To this day that young man tries to follow those instructions. He came to my office just recently, working on some alumni project. I truly believe that he learned something about the fact that "truth is stronger than fiction."

Take Truth Serum Regularly

Scientists are always experimenting with ideas and formulae and have developed in recent years what is called "truth serum." It is supposed to aid one in telling and recalling the truth. Its use at this time is not as impressive and extensive as other shots, vaccinations, and inoculations.

I am not sure that the world would be greatly served if such a serum were perfected. Why should human beings with the capacity to think, reason, and make moral and ethical judgments need to take a truth serum? On the other hand, criminal justice seems to be served significantly through the use of lie detectors. These tests are frequently administered by the police department, and general credence is given to the results.

There is a truth serum that can be taken that will assist in achieving the higher levels of honesty and morality. The serum is composed of several ingredients. Once these ingredients have been put together in what we might call a "serum," it is very important that the serum be taken properly and regularly.

Science has given us some of the components of the serum. It has established certain laws as true, others as false. It has unveiled knowledge relative to the operation of the physical universe. It has shown us the movement of the heavenly bodies and dissected a drop of water into molecules and atoms of innumerable quantity. The world of science contains a world of truth. We need to become well acquainted with it.

There are faith truths that need to go into the serum. These I shall refer to as immutable "whatsoever" truths. They come from the Word of God. The first is recorded in John 16:23, "Whatsoever ye shall ask the Father in my name, he will give it you." The second is in Galatians 6:7, "Be not deceived; God is not mocked: for whatsoever a man soweth, that shall he also reap." The third is in 1 Corinthians 10:31, "Whether therefore ye eat, or drink, or whatsoever ye do, do all to the glory of God."

There are love truths that need to go into this truth serum. These love truths are easy to recite but hard to live by. You and I have heard them the better part of our lives. In summary they are: love God, love your neighbor as yourself, love one another, husbands love your wives, wives love your husbands, children love and honor your parents, and love not the things of the world.

The last ingredient to go into the truth serum would be social truths. These are those eternal verities that really help make the world go around. Those verities are: the strong helping the weak, bearing one another's burden, extending a kind hand and warm heart to the stranger, mutual respect for each other, and individual freedom and competence.

Now that I have hurried through the enumeration of these ingredients of a good truth serum, let me suggest ways of taking the serum. Open-mindedness should always be practiced by the takers of the serum. A closed mind is not capable of discerning the truth and prevents the passage of truth into the heart just as a closed mouth prevents one from taking any kind of medicine. Sometimes tradition or experience tends to close the mind to new ideas, but truth must have free access to the mind. An open mind is not a mind that allows everything to go in and through it, but nothing remains. An open mind is one that approaches all truth with objectivity and candor. It is not bound by barnacles of habit or custom.

You are here on this planet Earth in quest for truth. Your quest will never end because all truth has not been discovered. Give yourself diligently to the search for truth. Live it, breathe it, obey it, and stand on it for the true way of life is the right way.

Truth is the real thing!

Notes

1. Harris Franklin Rall, *Christianity* (New York: Charles Scribner's Sons, 1941), pp. 129 *ff*.
2. T. DeWitt Talmage, *Sin* (Rhodes and McClure Publishing Company, 1901), p. 145.
3. William Cullen Bryant, "The Battlefield."

6

Seeking Out Options— You Do Have a Choice

When God created people he seemed to endow them with unusual traits, one of which is the power of choice. People are not puppets in the hands of a despotic God or victims of the laws of nature. God could have created people and so fashioned them that people would do everything in blind obedience to the will or wishes of God, but he chose not to do that because he wanted any obedience or loyalty that came from people to come voluntarily.

The power of choice is an awesome power. The difference in the right choice and the wrong choice is also awesome. Knowing what to choose, when to choose, and how to choose is not something that comes easy. It is very difficult to make decisions on a level higher than pure instinctive action. If I see a thrown object coming at me, such as a snowball, I duck and dodge the collision of the snowball upon my body. That is instinctive reaction. If, on the other hand, I become very angry at the person throwing the snowball and think about getting revenge, then there is a much more difficult decision to be made. Some of my choices are: throw a snowball at the culprit, shake my fist in his face, give him a tongue-lashing, or smile and go on my way. But any one of those decisions is more than an instinctive, self-preservation reaction for value judgments entered into whatever choice is made.

In making difficult choices one of the first reactions is, Why can't I do as I please?

Why Can't I Do as I Please?

My quick reaction to that question is, Please don't. You will be sorry if you do. I know that you, as well as I, tend to get tense and pressed by the decisions you have to make and the brevity of time you have in making those decisions. Ours is a life of quick decisions. We can't get away from the world or even go up into the mountains and sleep it off. Let us face our decisions with gratitude because we are not so regimented or controlled that someone else is making those decisions for us.

Now back to my original question, Why can't I do as I please about all my decisions? Freedom is the "in thing," isn't it? Most people feel like saying, "I gotta be me." Much has been made of the fact that every person is free and equal, but no two are alike. We all have that free spirit of not wanting to be fenced in. When I changed pastorates from Williamsburg, Kentucky, to Memphis, Tennessee, one of my good friends in Williamsburg was the chemistry professor of Cumberland College in that town. He came to me to share his parting feelings and said, "Well, I don't know anything about those people in Memphis, and I guess I will never know them as well as I know you, but I hope they won't fence you in." He was expressing a wish that I might be able to be free.

The child wants to be free to do as it pleases. Young people want no restraints. They want to be cut loose from Mom's apron strings as soon as possible. Adults want to be free to mind their own business and don't want to be bothered.

The greatest slavery in all the world is the slavery of self. Self is a good servant but a poor master. The tyrant of self is subject to every passion, whim, or fancy; thus it becomes unstable, unworthy of loyalty.

How can one do as one pleases in a world of four billion people? Just suppose that everyone passing through your city's airport was free to tell the air controllers when to instruct the pilots to take off and when to land the planes. Confusion, tragedy, and disaster would occur. Lives would be lost, planes would be destroyed, and no one would be effectively served. Suppose every student in school decided to do only that which pleased her; taking only the classes desired, coming to class only when convenient, and studying only that which was deemed relevant. What kind of educational and learning processes would occur? So no one is free to do as he or she pleases.

Usually the line of least resistance is followed when one persists in wanting to do as one pleases. It has been said of the Vikings, those hardy Norwegian sailors of earlier centuries, that the "north winds made the Vikings." They took the rough course. Of all the armor described in the Bible (see Eph. 6:10-20) for the Christian, there is nothing mentioned to cover the Christian's back, indicative that a Christian must always face the enemy and the currents.

Doing as I please might be pleasing but not proper and good. If a child is allowed to eat only sweets and nonnutritious foods, the child's health will be damaged. An unbalanced diet is detrimental to the health of a growing child. Our four-and one-half-year-old granddaughter was being urged by her grandmother to eat some green vegetable. Grandmother made a clear point that we all should try to eat something green each day. The granddaughter thought for a moment and then responded, "Grandmother, I think I will eat a green 'M & M' each day." I have seen this type of decision making transpire time and time again with high school and college students.

Thomas Huxley remarked that an educated person is one who "is able to make himself do what has to be done, when it is to be done, whether he likes it or not."

This infers that an educated person is not free to handle choices and options by doing as he pleases. Remember, Hitler, Napoleon, and Kaiser Wilhelm tried to do as they pleased. The outcome was fatal. Bad choices were made in each case—choices that were cruel, selfish, and gauged to satisfy their egos.

Four Inevitable Choices

You will be faced with four of the most important choices a person can make during the immediate years ahead of you. The choices are: Where will I get further educational preparation for life? What career do I wish to choose for my life? Who will be my companions and my life mate? and What will be my relationship to a church?

One can readily conclude that one choice is not as good as another in connection with these four choices. Careful selection must be involved. The consequence of each choice is extensive and far-reaching.

Not every person is totally free to choose an educational alma mater. This is true because of geography, economics, and educational desires. But a large percentage of high school graduates have the option of selecting the college of their choice. This is an important decision because in many cases the other three choices are made while one is in college. There are some 3,500 colleges and universities in the United States. There are public colleges and universities, private colleges and universities, and church-related colleges and universities. There is now within driving distance of almost every young person in the United States a college or university. All institutions of higher learning are not alike.

As you use your option of selecting a college or university, let me suggest five things. First, be sure that you select an institution that is academically sound, fully accredited by its accrediting agency. This will assure you of ease and capability in transferring your credits from one institution to another, as well as presenting you with solid academic offerings. Second, think about the size of the institution. Some are 40,000 in size while others go down to 400. A noted educator remarked, "A student who goes through a large college goes through more college, while one who attends a small college has more college go through the student."

Third, the cost and availability factors are not to be overlooked. Not everyone can afford financially to attend the "Ivy League" colleges. Not everyone would qualify scholastically to attend Harvard or Yale or other prestigious colleges.

Fourth, consider the private, church-related institutions. A church-related college has much to offer—academic excellence,

Christian emphasis, moral and ethical commitments, and a good student-teacher relationship. It has been said that more is caught than taught. This being the case, the instructor is important. Education is very costly and youth and parents should not take the choice of an alma mater lightly.

The fifth suggestion I would make is that you seek out the institution that can provide for you noble purposes, career goals, and religious commitments. Remember this whole matter of the selection of a college alma mater is not a question of public versus private or large versus small, but a question of personal choice. It is a question touching the deeper and more intangible realities of your life.

Your choice of a career or a profession in which you may use your talents and training is not something to wait out. Neither is it something that you might have arbitrarily forced upon you. One of the difficulties encountered by young people today in trying to choose a career is that there are so many different possibilities.

The college finds it very hard to train young people for jobs that don't exist now but will exist tomorrow. Even though the opportunities are multiple, let me offer you some basic guidelines in preparation for whatever may come to you.

First, be sure that you get a basic education as a good foundation to build on. Reading, writing, and arithmetic are still basic. The college degree is no longer the terminal degree for most persons, therefore it becomes more imperative that students take solid, basic courses while in college. The technical skills of a profession usually come in graduate school. It is important that a college graduate be able to speak correctly, think properly, make value judgments, know how to get along with people, and possess a work ethic. These attributes are basic in any skill, trade, or profession.

Second, try to determine what area of work would challenge you, call for the use of your talents, and provide for you a reasonable income. Work should be a pleasant privilege rather than a dull chore. There are many types of aptitude tests available to assist you in trying to determine just what area you might fit into.

Third, there may be a need for your services in particular areas, and those unmet needs may cause you to commit yourself to those areas. I feel, personally, that service is a very worthy and relevant factor in decision making.

Fourth, since God created you in his image, endowed you with many talents, you should seek his guidance as you search for your life's work. His power and presence throughout life can assist you greatly. Take him with you step by step.

Fifth, plan a program of continuing education. The explosion of knowledge demands that for persons to be efficient and effective they must read, study, and seek additional information. I am coming to feel that education beyond college is almost as important as the college educational experience. It should not be an either/or but a both/and career goal. There is no shortcut to success. There is no excelling without great labor and arduous study. Be a student all of your days on Earth.

Once you have chosen the college you wish to attend, you will immediately upon enrolling begin to make choices as to who your friends and companions will be while there. These are the folk you will live with, eat with, study with, and relax with day after day. They will have a great influence upon your life, and you in turn will have an influence upon them. You need to be very selective but not snobbish or proud. Study their life habits, their speech, and their self-control. Peer pressure is tremendous, and you must not be victimized by carelessly getting yourself into situations where the pressure leads you to do things you would not do otherwise. Students frequently give as excuses for their actions that they did it because others were doing it. A fine, stalwart young man said to me one day as we discussed matters of this nature, "I have decided that if I can't change the crowd, I will change crowds and not be changed by the crowd." It is good to be friendly with everyone, but you do not have to be a friend of everyone.

My advice would be to shun the groups which want everyone

to think alike, act alike, and dress alike. You can choose not to drink alcohol, not to smoke pot, and not to engage in premarital sex. These are choices you can control. It is not wise to engage in experimental activities of similar nature because habits are easily formed. Habits are difficult to break. I have never met a person who started to drink or smoke who intended to become addicted. In every case it was quite simple: there was the first time, maybe under peer pressure, and then the habit gradually took possession. Remember that every beginning has an end, every action a reaction. Peer-group action and morality are quite different from individual action and morality. The tendency of a group is to assert more freedom, less restraint, and at times concoct its own code of conduct.

Choose well both your individual and group friends, for some will remain your friends for a lifetime. Among these friends there is probably one very special friend of the opposite sex. God made us male and female. Love, courtship, marriage, and the family are a part of God's divine plan of the ages. In America we are not assigned husbands and wives by family or government. We are free to choose.

Let me suggest some attributes that I think our companions should have. There must be physical attractiveness and appeal. This is where the chemistry begins to flow.

While a high school student, I had a teacher who when the first time I saw her, I thought was the ugliest woman I had ever seen. Her features were not appealing. Her face and hair were lacking in natural beauty. But, lo and behold, before a month had gone by I thought that same teacher was one of the prettiest I ever sat under. What brought about such a drastic change? It was before the days of plastic surgery and face-lifts. She, more than anyone else, portrayed the saying, "Pretty is as pretty does." Her manners were charming. Her spirit and attitude were gentle and gracious. She exuded love for her students. Her spirit overpowered her looks. Looks are important but not everything.

Personality is a trait of vital significance. Personality is the expression of the soul, the inner person. There aren't many people who enjoy the company of a cynical, bitter, drab person. People enjoy people who glow and radiate love, concern, and appreciation.

Intelligence is another factor of concern. "Beautiful or handsome, but dumb" is out-of-date. An intelligent person is usually a good conversationalist, stimulating and enjoyable. Intelligence should never be used to establish superiority of one over the other, but used to pull out the best in each other.

Ideals and goals are ingredients to mix into the recipe for selecting a good companion. Friction appears instantly when one of high standards associates with one of low standards. It is not wise to compromise moral and ethical standards for popularity's sake. When this is done, whatever popularity might be gained becomes hollow and cheap. A happy, successful marriage is more than sexual gratification. It is the blending of two lives into one. The dance of two souls. There is sacrifice and give-and-take on both sides. I have felt through the years that if young people who are desperately in love, and who climax that love at the marriage altar, would work half as hard to make the marriage work as to get married, then all would be well. I want to share with you two experiences I have had with my wife of forty years, one before marriage and one just recently.

On one occasion before we were married I sent her eleven lovely red roses with the penned note, "Here are eleven lovely roses, and you are the twelfth lovelier than all the rest." That made quite a hit, and to my frugal blood eleven roses were cheaper than twelve. The point is: the price of a gift of shared love should be of minimal consequence, the feeling and intention of major consequence.

Recently, on the occasion of our fortieth wedding anniversary, I racked my brain to think of something to give my wife. Candy, flowers, clothes—all seemed inappropriate this time. Guess what? I called my groceryman-friend and asked, "Roy, will you fix me a box of forty delicious, choice, pink grapefruit?"

"Sure I will. When do you want them?" I went by the same afternoon and lugged the unattractive grocery box loaded with pink grapefruit into the house. My wife was pleased, amused, and most appreciative. It was not the cost which totaled $18.40, but the thought and feelings I had put into the deal. We both like grapefruit. They were really choice ones, the like of which we would not buy normally. The fruit was useful and very juicy and sweet (like my love for her).

Keep your love life growing and glowing with thoughtful and considerate deeds of love. Choose well your companions and especially that one with whom you will share the bedroom, the dining room, the living room, the yard, and vacation days.

There is one other major choice that you will need to consider during your days of "meeting the challenge." You have the option of investing your life in worthwhile worship activities and Christian services through a local church. The church is not like any other organization or club. Its founding, its purpose, its membership, and its practices are different. The Christian church was founded by Jesus Christ. He founded it to perpetuate his plans and to provide for his followers a place of fellowship and function. That church now has millions of congregations of various denominations meeting primarily on Sundays to honor the name of Christ and to carry out his mission. No institution has made as great a contribution to civilization as the church. Its message of love and redemption through God's Son, Christ, and its program of love for one's neighbor as oneself have been reflected in millions of lives. Humanitarian agencies and institutions, such as orphanages, hospitals, women's rights, mission activities, and care of the needy have sprung from the church. It merits loyalty, if for no other reason, because of its unparalleled contribution to society and in particular to Western civilization. No one can ever repay it for these things.

The church offers the individual opportunities of personal confrontation and commitment to the higher values of life. No other club or agency does this. Where else can one go and be confronted with the message of sin, its wages and penalty, and at the same time be offered a message of hope, forgiveness, and eternal life? Sooner or later everyone must face up to his or her personal relationship to God in Christ. The church stands ever ready to proclaim that message of mercy and grace. The church keeps a constant challenge of loving and sharing before the members. Do not pass it by or leave your participation in it to a later time. You need the church, and the church needs you.

7

Working, Working, Working

Life is work, and work is life. Thank God that's the way it is. Wouldn't you hate to be born with nothing to do but fritter away time until death? I have a strong feeling that doing nothing would be far worse than doing something.

Did you ever stop to think that God is still working? He not only created the heavens and earth and everything that is in them, humanity included, but also he works constantly. You and I put a lot of work upon him. We implore him with our prayers and hope he is listening. We ask for his guidance and trust he will go with us. We pray for his presence as the Great Physician when our loved ones are ill, and we know he is there. Occasionally, we think about thanking him, and we are grateful he has time to hear us. The following couplet describes additional activities of God:

> My Lord, he knows all I do; he hears all I say;
> he's just a-writing all the time.

This plus the fact that not a sparrow falls to ground without the Father's knowledge (Matt. 10:29) shows us how busy he really is, and, if the hairs of our heads are numbered, God has some extra work to do keeping up with mine because I'm losing my hair rapidly in my latter days.

It's the Principle of Life

Since Adam and Eve were ordered out of the Garden of Eden we have had to earn our living by the sweat of our brow, and that is not too bad. Even though the mandate "work or starve" is strong, that doesn't make work a blight or a burden.

Stop to think for a moment. The average person will spend more of a lifetime working than doing anything else unless it is sleeping, and sleeping is just rebuilding for more work. Some people also try to sleep on the job. Have you heard of the night watchman who, when he said, "Last night I dreamed that . . .," got fired from his job? Or think of Rip Van Winkle who went up into the mountain and slept for twenty years. He slept through a revolution and missed some momentous hours in the history of our nation. Work and sleep are complementary to each other, not a substitute for each other, and both should be equally pleasant.

"The Skylark's Bargain" is a poem about a foolish and lazy skylark who was willing to sell his feathers for worms. Doing it that way made life come easy for the moment. The skylark felt he had stumbled upon a good thing, that luck was coming just at the right time. No more digging and grubbing for worms. No more getting up early to become an early bird in order to get worms. All that the skylark had to do was pluck out a feather when he wanted a worm.

> Who will buy? Who will buy?
> I am selling in all weathers
> Fine and fat and juicy worms
> In exchange for skylark's feathers.
>
> Who will buy? Who will buy?
> Surely we can come to terms
> In exchange for skylark's feathers
> I am selling luscious worms.
>
> Here lies a foolish skylark,
> Hush your note each bird that sings,
> Here lies a poor lost skylark,
> Who for earthworms sold his wings.[1]

You might respond by saying, "Well, no person would sell his life to keep from working." Are you sure? I was working with a young man twenty-five years ago who would sell his blood in order to get money to buy alcohol, and alcohol was ruining his life. I have known other young people who would sell good opportunities for a little bit of security or ease.

Feathers for the skylark are for flying and soaring, not for earthworms.

Kenneth Kaufman wrote a poem entitled "Tame Duck" which points out the necessity of working and striving for the high lanes:

> I think myself a tame old duck
> Dabbling around in barnyard muck,
> Fat and lazy with useless wings;
> But sometimes when the northwind sings,
> And the wild ones hurtle overhead,
> It remembers something lost and dead,
> And cocks a wary, bewildered eye,
> And makes a feeble attempt to fly.
> It's fairly content with the shape it's in,
> But it isn't the duck it might have been.

So, feathers are useful for ducks and skylarks, and work is useful for persons. But I hope you will see the lessons to be learned from these two little poems about the foolish skylark and the tame duck and resolve to go on working, working, working. A Dutch proverb tells us, "Laziness goes so slow that poverty overtakes it."

Think of your work in science as the discovery of new things; your work in language as the opportunity to get acquainted with a new tongue, a new people, a new culture; your work in literature as sharing an evening with the great minds of the yesteryears; and your studies in history as partially reconstructing the past. It's mostly all a matter of how you approach your work, how you view it, and how you cast it into your mind and soul. Instead of working like slaves, we could work like princes. Whatever you are doing, think of it as an essential part of your growth and development in earning a livelihood; think of it as providing something for someone else; and think of it as part of your own self-fulfillment.

So it is a law of nature: "work or starve," starve mentally, starve physically, starve morally; but work and live happily, live healthfully, live helpfully. It is a well-known fact that more people break down from worry and dissipation than from overwork, or another way of saying it is that more people rust out than wear out.

It Adds Pleasure to Life

I am going to make a very drastic statement that I feel is true. If work does not add pleasure to life, then there is no pleasure in life. Do you believe it? If there is no pleasure in work, then all of the ancillary activities engaged in for pleasure are not and will not be adequate to cancel out the drudgery of work. So then the "biggie" is: how can I get pleasure out of my work?

There are at least three vital aspects of work that will, when present, enhance the pleasure of work. The first of these is pride in one's work. Whether the work is classroom work, manual labor, office work, housework, or some highly skilled professional job, each task should be discharged with a sense of pride. Pride comes from a feeling that we have done our best, that our efforts are important and that we have taken a particular interest in doing our part.

Two men boarded a ferryboat to go to the other side of a stream. Upon boarding the little junket they noticed an old, black man cleaning and polishing the motor of the boat. He took particular pride in what he was doing, smiling all the time. At first his work appeared to the strangers to be nothing more than busy work. But they sensed a deep concern on the old man's face for what he was doing. One of the men, feeling even more curious as the motor began to putter, knowing that it would soon be greasy again, sidled up to the river captain and said, "Sir, I have noticed how carefully you have cleaned and shined the motor of your boat. Won't it soon be dirty again? Isn't that useless work?"

"Oh, no Sir, it is not useless work for you see, I'se got a glory in my work. I am proud of this little boat, its motor, and the opportunity I have to ferry folks across this stream." A glory in one's work is equal to pleasure in work.

Wouldn't all classroom work be more pleasurable if every assignment could be approached with a feeling of "I'se got a glory" in doing that assignment. After all, everything written or spoken by students indicates either peripherally or very pointedly the amount of pride taken by the student in classroom recitation and term papers composed.

A second quality that will enhance work comes from approaching work with a sense of service rendered, a sense of achievement, and a sense of fulfillment. This type of approach puts a personal stamp upon our work. It is our personal "watermark" woven into the product which consumes our time.

Margaret Fuller, an American author, critic, and feminist of the early nineteenth century, remarked that she "accepted the universe." Someone reported that to Thomas Carlyle, the famed essayist of the same century, and he remarked, "Gad, she'd better!" But, someone else hearing both remarks retorted, "Gad, she'd better not!" Betterment of life is the story of those who through patient and sacrificial labor would not accept things as they are, but strive to make them better and more self-fulfilling.

A sense of pride and fulfillment seems to be a part of children. Who has not seen a child making something out of modeling clay? The observer may not recognize the object as what the child calls it, but the imagination of the child called for self-achievement and approval.

Bricklaying can be just laying brick. It also can be considered an essential part of a building, or it can be considered the vital part of a cathedral in which men and women will worship and honor God. A farmer may consider the harvesting of his crops just another part of his yearlong work, or he can think of his efforts as providing meat, bread, and vegetables for the consumer. Pride, achievement, and self-fulfillment add pleasure to all work.

Why not smile as you work? It takes fewer muscles to smile

than to frown. Sing at work, if not aloud, inwardly. Joy is a great pacifier and stimulus to energy. Whistle at times. Instead of whistling in the dark, whistle away the dark days and low moments.

The third quality to work that adds great pleasure to life comes when we feel that we have been adequately compensated for our efforts. I know you and I feel at times that our compensation is not adequate, but on second thought we both may be faring better than we deserve. Some years ago a questionnaire sent to a group of wage earners asked the question, "What amount would it take to make you pleased with your job?" The majority said an increase of one-third would be minimal. I wonder if we aren't of the nature and disposition that, if the one-third increase were given, we would not soon thereafter expect another one-third increase because monetary income never seems to satisfy.

Working Give Profits to Life

If we are always working, working, working, there are many profits that will come to life. One of these is adequate compensation. I have told our students over the years that they will get paid more for doing what they are not paid to do than for doing only that which they are paid to do. Extra time given without pay will produce rich dividends down the road. There can be no excelling without great labor. Elbert Hubbard put it this way, "Folks who never do any more than they get paid for, never get paid for any more than they do." Charles M. Schwab, one of the greatest salesmen America ever produced, said, "The man who does not work for the love of work but only for money is not likely to make money nor to find much fun in life." Money cannot buy happiness, health, or a good homelife. Lusting for it can destroy all three of these. Remember, money does not grow on trees, nor does it grow on sprees. It is the reward of labor that is sometimes long, sometimes hard, and often fun.

Working, working, working will not only produce a good income for the worker but will also provide moments of inspiration. Inspiration comes after perspiration. Many of the great masterpieces in music, art, and science have come in "flash moments" to persons like Edison, Tchaikovsky, and Madame Curie after they had prodigiously plodded day and night seemingly without success.

Working, working, working has a good curative effect upon the body. Tension, stress, idleness tend to cause the forces of the mind, body, and soul to work against each other. Health has come again and again to those who have lost themselves in gainful, pleasant employment. It may not be possible always to choose one's day-to-day activities, but one always has the privilege of engaging in those activities with an engaging enthusiasm and an optimistic spirit.

Serendipities Are Unusual Spinoffs of Working, Working, Working

Horace Walpole, the author of nearly 3,000 witty, charming letters, coined the word *serendipity*. He got the idea from the tale of the *Three Princes of Serendip*, Ceylon, who, in their travels, were always discovering, by chance more than by sagacity, pleasant things they did not seek.

Columbus, seeking a better route to Asia, stumbled upon America.

Pasteur, working with wine that would turn sour, discovered pasteurization.

Graham Bell, seeking to improve the telegraph, got the telephone.

Roentgen, working on better light for photography, got on the trail of X ray, the Roentgen ray.

A chemist, who had grains of rice in a test tube over a flame, dropped the tube and rice exploded. Thus he got puffed rice.

The famous Dead Sea Scrolls, found in the Qumran area of Palestine, were discovered by a shepherd lad who was tending the sheep. One of the sheep disappeared into an opening in the rock, and the lad tossed in a stone hoping to cause the animal to come out. He heard a crash and entered the opening to find a broken jar that was stuffed with precious scrolls of biblical significance.

And so, life has produced serendipities galore.

Working, working, working will provide some serendipities for those who diligently pursue their tasks. I would like to mention at least four. First, luck, as I define it, will come to those who work the hardest. I am not sure there is any such thing as luck as commonly thought of: the chance happening of events unexpected and unplanned. If you will define luck as that which is born of the use of good mental powers, impregnated with hardships and trials, and energized with a good physical output, then I am a 100 percent believer. Benjamin Franklin said that "diligence is the mother of luck." We can make our breaks. We are not condemned to ill luck, nor are we blessed with lucky stars.

Second, another serendipity coming from working, working, working, is that there is a possibility a few might become geniuses. A great philosopher once said, "When I hear a young man spoken of as giving promise of high genius, the first question I ask about is, always, 'Does he work?'"

The third serendipity that may emerge from hard and pleasant work is something I choose to call "Open Sesame." This is a term coming from the Arabian Nights' tale of *Ali Baba and the Forty Thieves*. It was the magical command that opened the door of the robbers' den and has come to mean something that unfailingly opens. I have a sister who was a nurse for about thirty-five years, retiring several years ago. One day during her early days as a nurse, while working in the emergency ward at the hospital, she found herself assisting two doctors who were putting a pin in a patient's knee. She had not seen the doctors before. They seemed to her to be rather stern, impatient, and demanding. She did the best she could with a smile. She was glad when the work was completed and a bit downcast because she thought she had rendered mediocre service as an assistant to the doctors. There was a feeling inside that tilted toward a hope that she would not be asked to work with the same two again. Two weeks passed, and she received a phone call from those two doctors. They asked her to come to their clinic. She went out of courtesy only to be greeted most cordially. They told her that they were impressed with her assistance and spirit on that particular day. She was asked to join their clinic and she did, with a significant increase in salary and a longtime good relationship with them. The first experience with the doctors became an "open sesame" for my sister.

Finally, working, working, working will frequently provide a serendipity which I choose to call "Millionaire of Distinction." I much prefer this title to one which appears occasionally in newspaper advertisements designated as "men of distinction." The paradox of that designation is that people who use the product advertised—liquor—more realistically sometimes become "men of extinction." The person who aligns all his mental powers, physical powers, ambition, enthusiasm, and dependability is likely to become a millionaire of distinction. And, incidentally, quite a few achieve the million dollar status.

As I see it then, the "happy hour" is not the occasion when people gather and drink alcoholic beverages because those hours usually eventuate into abnormal speech and action for the one created in the image of God, but the happy hour is the hour of the day when one can see in review that he has done his best in the best way possible for the good of all.

Note

1. From LISTEN, MY CHILDREN by Herbert K. England copyright © 1944, renewed 1972 by Herbert K. England. Published by Fleming H. Revell Company. Used by permission.

8

Watching the Clock

Most people can be called "clock-eyed persons," clock-watchers. We look at the clock because we are conscious of time. The only equality is the equality of time. All have the present moment which cannot be divided, saved for a rainy day, or stored away. We talk about "killing time," "wasting time," "making time," and "spending time." What we are actually saying is that we can do something with the present moment. There is no way to call back a passed moment or a wasted minute, nor any way to call forth one on deposit for the future. Benjamin Franklin, noted for so many sayings, said, "Time: the stuff life is made of." Since that is the case, watching the clock that registers the time of the day is also watching our life's activities registered each day.

What Is Time?

Time has been defined as a segment of movement, motion, or the period between two events. More specifically time has been broken down into seconds, minutes, hours, days, years, a lifetime, a thousand years, and eternity. This facilitates record keeping and establishes a relationship between events.

There are many unanswered philosophical questions relating to time. When did time begin? Where did time come from? How much time is there? Where does time go?

From our human perspective, time seems boundless—no beginning and no ending. When we speak of the "beginning of time," we refer to the beginning of recorded time. Time began for each one of us at birth for that is the time we were certified as having been born an individual. From that point onward each person lives a moment at a time, and the activities are recorded on what I choose to call "time's calendar."

No one knows when time, as we define it, began nor when it will end. It flows like a river that has no beginning or end. Time and tide wait for no one, and each person must move with the flow of time to take full advantage of it.

How much time is there? Well, who knows? There is enough time, and there always will be enough time for each event to occur in the divine plan of the ages. God, who is the author of time, is not short of time. When the question, How much time is there? relates to you and me, then that is a different matter. Our time on earth is known only to God. We must live one day at a time. We may have several years left, or the time for our departure may be close at hand. Living, therefore, one day at a time means that we should live each day as if it were the last one. One thing is sure, we have the present; and that is all the time we can use properly.

Where does time go? It doesn't depart for it is an endless stream. Yesterday doesn't flow into today, and today doesn't flow into tomorrow; for when these things occur, it is present time. Time just goes on and on. It is infinite motion without a moment of rest. Our interpretations of this motion of time make it appear to be elastic. Some days stretch out with seeming endlessness; others jet by like a flash. An hour spent at the hospital awaiting the outcome of surgery on a loved one may seem like an eternity while to a couple in love, an hour is gone before it seemingly started. This is the difference in what we call *measured* and *felt duration* of time, for it seems to move sometimes quickly and sometimes slowly.

Time has been classified into three segments: past, present, and future. Augustine spoke of the three segments of time:

> At any rate it is now quite clear that neither future nor past actually exists. Nor is it right to say there are three times, past, present and future. Perhaps it would be more correct to say: there are three times, a present of things past, a present of things

present, and a present of things future. For these three exist in the mind and I find them nowhere else: the present of things past is memory, the present of things present is sight, the present of things future is expectation.[1]

If Augustine is correct, and I am not disposed to take issue with him, then we live with the three elements of time ever with us: memory of the past, present of things in sight, and present expectations of the future.

What Time Is It?

Go ahead and look at your watch, but I am afraid that will only give you the time of the day. No one knows what time it is with reference to the world or individual life. We know only that the time is the present. It is now.

An elderly husband woke his wife late one evening and said with a startling voice, "Wake up, honey, it is later than it has been in the history of the world. The clock has just struck sixteen times." Maybe it is later than we think. At least there are no minutes to waste, and time truly marches on. Samuel Johnson had engraved on his watch, "It is later than you think." Walter Scott had that statement on his sun dial. Coleridge stated it in one of his books, and a devout Christian had it on a seal with which he stamped all of his letters.

If it is later than we think, it is time to get busy. *It is time to take out the garbage* that may be residing in our minds. Thoughts of envy, jealousy, and hatred need to be dumped now before they do more harm. A spirit of gloom and doom needs to be carried to the dump heap. All of those negative thoughts are too time consuming. Let us dump them on the garbage heap.

When I was in high school during the early thirties, I experienced something that wanted to cling in my mind. The high school was a county high school located at Smith Mills, Kentucky, in the western part of the state. It was a small school with limited facilities. We carried our lunch and at noon found some time to play basketball if we removed the portable stage. One winter day at lunch, while we were gathered around a potbellied stove, Wallace said to Sam, "I dare you to spit on Herbert." My name is Herbert, and Sam was very accurate with his spital. But when spital landed on me something landed in my mind—a thought of revenge. I couldn't take Sam on, for he was much bigger than I; and Wallace, his buddy, was bigger and stronger than either of us. I felt, however, that my time would come, and come it did a few days later.

We were playing basketball, and I was fast and light on my feet whereas Sam was fat and clumsy. He came dribbling the ball down the floor, and I saw my one grand opportunity to square the deal. I quickly threw out my foot, tripping him. He headed toward the goal in an horizontal position, and I watched him with glee until he arose with a scowl on his face. At that moment, I took off, knowing that he wouldn't catch me. Up and down the steps we went. I was getting away from him. Suddenly, one of my friends appeared and told me to stop running. When Sam caught up with me, the friend said to Sam, "Listen, don't you ever lay a hand on Herbert. If you do, I'll take care of you." Nothing else happened as a result of that experience during my years in high school. I couldn't forget it, however.

In 1957 I was asked to deliver the annual message at the meeting of the Tennessee Baptist Convention. I chose as my subject "The Relevance of an Impossible Ideal." My mind went back to that high school experience and to the passage in Matthew 5:44 where Jesus said, "I say unto you, Love your enemies, bless them that curse you, do good to them that hate you." The thought of Sam and that Scripture passage could not inhabit the same mind. Loving one's enemy seemed an impossible ideal, so I dumped the hatred toward Sam that had lodged in my heart through the years and replaced it with love and forgiveness.

It is time to deliver the daily paper, the Word of God, with the front-page story that there is good news and a good life for those who will heed the admonitions of Christ. That wonderful news is recorded in the Gospel of Matthew, chapters 5—7, which tells us how to make the most of time and how to major on the things that really count and transcend time. Take a Bible and read those chapters right now.

Since it is later than we think, it is time to *buy up the opportunities that are around.* Opportunities are the "best stocks" available. They are blue-chip stocks with a good dividend return. The apostle Paul wrote to his friends in Ephesus, "See then that ye walk circumspectly, not as fools, but as wise, Redeeming the time [buying up opportunities—a better translation], because the days are evil" (Eph. 5:15-16). Opportunities of self-investment abound for the alive-eyed person. Opportunities for service are everywhere. How about trying to go the second mile in your work? How about trying to give yourself away? How about trying to seize a chance for self-improvement as it flies by? Your school library has many good books that will, upon reading, unveil some opportunities you can follow through on.

Buy up the opportunity to say something good about your friends, your school, and your company. Try today to express to someone your heartfelt gratitude for some favor shown you or some good deed done by that friend. Follow the advice of the poet who wrote, "Count that day lost, whose low descending sun/Views from thy hand no worthy action done."

It is time to buy up your dreams. If dreams were for sale, what would you buy? It is good that you can dream, and I trust you have dreams deeply implanted in your soul. Several years ago a popular song had words like these, "And if I am dreaming, just let me dream on." Too much day-dreaming is bad. Dreams have no value unless they produce in the dreamer a creativeness and discipline that will put mind, soul, and energy into the commitment to bringing those dreams to pass. The brains of the dreamers have wrought many human miracles. Dreamers have fought and died for bigger things than jeweled crowns and higher seats than golden thrones. They are the architects of greatness. Their vision lies within their souls. They peer beyond the veil and mist of doubt and despair and pierce the high walls of unborn time. Dream of the heights and start now an assault of the hills.

It is later than you think, well into the morning, and it *is time to go jogging.*

Rudyard Kipling wrote a beautiful poem entitled *If*:

> If you can keep your head when all about you
>   Are losing theirs and blaming it on you,
> If you can trust yourself when all men doubt you,
>   But make allowance for their doubting too;
> If you can wait and not be tired by waiting,
>   Or being lied about, don't deal in lies,
> Or being hated, don't give way to hating,
>   And yet don't look too good, nor talk too wise:
>
> If you can dream—and not make dreams your master;
>   If you can think—and not make thoughts your aim;
> If you can meet with Triumph and Disaster
>   And treat those two impostors just the same;
> If you can bear to hear the truth you've spoken
>   Twisted by knaves to make a trap for fools,
> Or watch the things you gave your life to, broken,
>   And stoop and build 'em up with worn-out tools:
>
> If you can make one heap of all your winnings
>   And risk it on one turn of pitch-and-toss,
> And lose, and start again at your beginnings
>   And never breathe a word about your loss;
> If you can force your heart and nerve and sinew
>   To serve your turn long after they are gone,
> And so hold on when there is nothing in you
>   Except the Will which says to them: "Hold on!"
>
> If you can talk with crowds and keep your virtue,
>   Or walk with Kings—nor lose the common touch,
> If neither foes nor loving friends can hurt you,
>   If all men count with you, but none too much;
> If you can fill the unforgiving minute
>   With sixty seconds' worth of distance run,
> Yours is the Earth and everything that's in it,
>   And—which is more—you'll be a Man, my son!

Commit it to memory and say it at least once a week. If you are a jogger, say it as you are jogging.

Tackle each job and each opportunity with a sense of urgency. Imagine that time is looking over your shoulder and holding the watch on your jog through life. Pace yourself through life. Run with patience and courage. One of the saddest of all lines is the line that says, "Well, it might have been, but time is now gone."

Are You Having a Good Time?

Usually when we think of a good time, we think of a period of time when persons gather for relaxation, pleasure, and sometimes frivolity. I am thinking in a more serious vein about making good time in good living.

Among the many things essential in making good time in good living, three are the most important. First, consider the fact that life must be lived within the limits of time, and time takes no holiday. Ralph Sockman, in his book *A Lift For Living*, tells of the late President Faunce of Brown University speaking to his students on the subject "The Pleasures of Economy." President Faunce pointed out: "In games and sports, one source of pleasure is in the limitation imposed. In baseball, for example, the player is allowed only three strikes. If the batter were permitted to strike at the ball as long as he pleased, the game would become too dull for the players or the spectators.

"In golf a player is allowed one little ball and one drive at a time. If he could keep on driving until he got a drive which satisfied him, nobody would care to play with him. In fact, some of us would never get off the first tee!

"Similarly, life is a game which has to be played within the limits of time."[2]

No one can afford, therefore, to waste time. Time wasted can never be bought back. I know of no place where time is for sale. I know of no market where bundles of time can be purchased. Once it is gone, it is gone forever.

Second, consider the economy of time. Even an hour every day for ten to twelve years will transform anyone with ordinary ability from ignorance to learning. Take an hour a day for three hundred days a year for ten years, and you would spend three thousand golden hours. Spend those hours toward some specific end, and the results will be amazing.

The United States government, with its gold stored at Fort Knox, Kentucky, requires the very dust of its storage rooms to be gathered up for the few grains of gold that may thus be saved. Could we not learn from this the nobler economy of time? Should we not glean every spare moment we have, knowing that each grain of time is valuable. A Chinese proverb further underscores this truth: "A lost inch of gold may be found, a lost inch of time—never." Try not to lose moments between sunrise and sunset.

Lost wealth, lost money, and lost health might be replaced, but lost time can never be redeemed.

Third, consider asking for something extra to do in order to have a good time in life. It is important to stay busy so that laziness and idleness won't take over. I have read an allegorical tale about a man who died and went into another world. There he had everything he wanted. He had nothing to do. He had servants at his bidding. Every time he had a wish someone was always near to grant that wish. Day after day he reveled in such elegant treatment. Slowly, however, he became a bit bored; then he became tired and fretful. He finally asked someone for something to do and was told that he could not have that wish granted. In desperation and frustration he blurted out, "Well, I wish I had gone to hell when I died."

Quickly the reply came back, "Where do you think you are?"

It would be hell to have nothing to do. Hell in this life and hell in the next life. Working within the context of time brings pleasure and joy. In heaven we shall be very active—"He that is righteous, let him be righteous still: and he that is holy, let him be holy still" (Rev. 22:11).

Shakespeare had King Richard say, "I wasted time, and now doth time waste me."

So look around, search the world over, ask for something to do if time hangs heavy with you. Don't waste it. Develop the art of making good time in good living. (You may want to read Ecclesiastes 3:1-8.)

Notes

1. Augustine, *Augustine's Confessions*, XI 20.
2. Ralph W. Sockman, *A Lift for Living* (New York: Abingdon, 1956), p. 131.

Section III
Where Do I Go from Here?

A companion question to Where do I go from here? is, Where do I want to go? There are in this world many interesting and exotic places. There are many attractive jobs and professions. There are crowds all along the way. There are also many enticements seeking to lure the traveler on to side roads.

Drifting is subject to the currents. In order to avoid drifting, chart a course for your pilgrimage. Make yourself a road map. Strive earnestly to stay on course. My successor as president of Belmont College, Dr. William E. Troutt, decided early in life that someday he would like to be a college president. He got the best training he could in preparation for such a position. He sought employment that would give him good experience to be an educational administrator. He worked consecutively for a local college, the state Higher Education Commission, a national educational consulting firm, and then as executive vice-president of the college which elected him president. He stayed on course and at the age of thirty-three became one of the youngest college presidents in the nation.

Exotic places like El Dorado, Treasure Island, or the fountain of youth exist only in the mind but have their counterparts in today's world. Beware lest the allurements of those glittering calls detour you away from your goal. Read the story of the prodigal son in Luke 15:11-32.

There are many crossroads in life. A theologian-philosopher imagined a person at the crossroads of life being tugged two ways. God from above looked down and tugged, and Satan looked up and tugged. The person's effort would make the

101

difference as to which way might be chosen.

You will inevitably go through the valley of doubt and, hopefully, into faithland; you will need to enroll in the university of experience; and you will eventually turn your face toward the land of beginning again. This will be a glorious sight as you face and meet the challenge.

9

Through the Valley of Doubt into Faithland

The pilgrimage of life goes through the valley of doubt and hopefully to the borders of faithland. The time the pilgrim spends in the valley of doubt is self-determined. Entrance into that area which I have chosen to call "faithland" is also a decisional experience that can be made only by the pilgrim.

No one has ever said and no promises have ever been made describing life as nothing but a "bed of roses." There are valleys and there are hills, valleys of doubt and despair and hills of hope and conquest. The valleys are as important as the hills. If life were all valleys, it would produce despair, despondency, blurred vision, and gloom. If life were all hills, it would be life with no challenges, weakened by the altitude and thinness of the air. Valleys are frequently far more productive than the hills and make possible the urge, the means, and the desire to scale the hills.

I Doubt It

Doubts are inevitable, inescapable. I doubt if there is a person who has not at some time or other experienced doubts. And that's not all bad. Have we not felt a little shaky, doubtful, about the merits of goodness as opposed to evil when on every hand evil seems to triumph? Have we ever doubted the efficacy of prayer? Most of us have probably thought, at one time or another, *I don't see any need of praying. God doesn't have time to hear me. He is too busy, and I am too inconsequential.* Maybe there has been some doubt as to the existence of God, especially as a personal God interested in persons. Can we claim any kinship with doubting Thomas? These doubts may cause us to question the sincerity of our preachers and teachers, the integrity of our leaders, and the love of our family.

Don't walk away from doubt. Don't be afraid of it. Don't condemn yourself for having doubts.

A doubt can be in the nature of inquiry or inquisitiveness. It can be wholly justified, and it can serve a good purpose. The world today is a better world because people of science and vision doubted the status quo and questioned and explored.

Sometimes doubt is the response to intuition. Shakespeare said, "Modest doubt is called the beacon of the wise—the tent that searches to the bottom of the worst." It is an incentive to search for truth and may well lead the way to truth. It may well be the corridor through which the seeker must pass in order to enter the chamber of vision.

Granted that doubts are inevitable and granted that doubts have assailed us, it is time to take a solid look at these doubts.

I Will Look at My Doubts

You may say, "I want to look at my doubts honestly and fairly." Good for you! Believe me when I say that some hot-headed youth assume positions from which they often stubbornly refuse to retreat.

Doubts may easily arise from a lack of knowledge. It is easier to doubt the veracity of something with which we are unfamiliar than it is to throw a question mark at that with which we are familiar and conversant. It is easier to believe in things that can be felt, touched, and tasted than to believe in the invisible, the intangible.

Feelings and thoughts gained in childhood may haunt us throughout life and cause us to go on doubting. I tried to minister to a very lovely lady—wealthy, charming, gracious, and generous—who said to me several times that she was in doubt about the certainty of her religious faith. We talked hours on end, and finally she told me that once she, an energetic and inquisitive child, was told by an older relative, "My dear child, you are so active and inquiring that you don't know and I am not sure that you are one of God's children." The recollection of that careless, inappropriate remark had lodged in her mind and haunted her day and night.

One's physical condition may produce doubt. Those who are tired, sick, and depressed frequently question the goodness of God. They are very prone to ask, Why did this happen to me? Why can't I be like others?

Young people are more likely to ask questions than any other group of people. You are no longer accepting without question what your parents have said or are saying. You are thinking for yourselves. You have new freedom of thought, expression, and independence. On the college level, you have come into a circle composed of those who have just come from home and those who have been away two to four years. College age is a questioning age, and rightly so. Science opens students' eyes to the boundless visible and invisible world appearing to the student as being almost self-sufficient. Philosophy opens doors of truth and inquiry never before relevant to the student. And on and on we could go.

Years ago Professor Simon Greenleaf, once an atheist, taught in the department of evidence at Harvard Law School. He came to the conclusion that, since the resurrection is the keystone in the arch of the Christian faith, he would submit the evidence of the resurrection to the same tests to which evidence in court must be submitted before it becomes admissible and credible testimony in court. He had a twofold purpose: he wanted to prove the unreliability of the witnesses, and he then would write a book that would disprove the resurrection of Jesus Christ. Greenleaf was honest in his research and did not try to make the research arbitrarily fit his personal beliefs. To his utter astonishment, he found that, even under the severest tests, the witnesses were credible and accurate. He arrived at a conclusion which was the opposite of the one he had hoped to arrive at: the resurrection of Jesus is a fact, and Jesus did come from the tomb. In the end Greenleaf wrote a book, one of the greatest of all times, attesting to the truth of the death, burial, and resurrection of Jesus. Greenleaf doubted, sought an answer, and followed truth.[1]

With a sense of urgency and with integrity, look at your doubts. Place them under careful scrutiny. Gather all the available facts. Search for the experiences of others. Seek counsel from those you respect and admire. You may find your question marks giving way to exclamation marks of affirmation.

I May Doubt My Doubts

All doubts don't give way to certainty. In the process of resolution, some may be cleared more quickly than others. Some may very stubbornly remain. The process may be soul stirring and upsetting. The progress from doubt to faith is frequently tedious and trying.

Alfred Lord Tennyson was the best-loved poet of his time. Have you ever read his poem *In Memoriam*? A more correct title of that poem would be *In Memoriam A.H.H.* Do you remember what the initials A.H.H. stood for? Those initials stood for the name of his friend, Arthur Henry Hallam, who died at the age of twenty-two. Hallam met Tennyson at Trinity College, Cambridge, in 1829, and there was established an ever-memorable friendship. The untimely death of Hallam and new scientific discoveries called Tennyson's religious faith and the faith of his age into question. Tennyson fought those doubts in his soul. Why did Hallam die so young? What does faith say? For ten years after Hallam's death, Tennyson published nothing. The death of his friend was the most profound emotional shock he ever experienced. He fought his way through doubt, despair, questioning and came to write the poem as a plea for faith out of doubt. Here are some of his words:

> Strong Son of God, immortal Love,
>   Whom we, that have not seen thy face,
>   By faith, and faith alone, embrace
> Believing where we cannot prove;

. . . .

Our wills are ours, we know not how;
Our wills are ours, to make them thine.

Tennyson truly faced his doubts but came to an affirmation of faith in God unequaled in the annals of poetry.

Fight your battles in the valley of doubt, fight with all your might, then plunge forward into faithland. There is light at the end of the tunnel. Give attention to your doubts. Handle them with skill and care. Go for the truth. Heed the admonition of Caleb Colton: "When we are in doubt and puzzle out the truth by our own exertions, we have gained something that will stay by us and will serve us again—But if to avoid the trouble of the search we avail ourselves solely of the superior information of a friend, such knowledge will not remain with us; we have not bought, but borrowed it."[2]

I Will Believe My Beliefs

It has been said that unless we "doubt our doubts and believe our beliefs, soon we will doubt our beliefs and believe our doubts." Faith grows much stronger through constant affirmation.

Some have inferred that life is a gamble and Christian faith is betting one's life that there is a God. These odds are in favor of the gambler: "For the earth is the Lord's, and the fulness thereof" (1 Cor. 10:26), and "The heavens declare the glory of God; and the firmament sheweth his handiwork" (Ps. 19:1).

In strengthening one's beliefs, four things can be very helpful. First, fasten some basic beliefs to a tether pole in your mind and never become disassociated from those truths. Know some things for "keeps." Tie your Christian beliefs, your scientific knowledge, and the basic fundamental truths of the universe to that tether pole and work your way out to the circumference. Accept the Bible as the Word of God and carry your questions of doubt to that treasury of truth. Measure the temporal by the eternal.

A second helpful procedure is to search for light at every

possible source. Look at things in their historical perspective and context. Seek the wisdom from the past. Pull all of the present light possible upon the problem. Shove aside all your biases and prejudices. With an open mind and a questing heart, go for the center of the matter. Don't be daunted by not being able to see all the way through the problem at first. I have never gotten in my car at night and decided against going someplace because when I started the motor and turned on the car lights I could not see around the first corner. Car lights project about three hundred feet in front of the car. As the car proceeds around the corner, the lights move with the car, lighting the road ahead. So it is with our quest for truth and light. Step by step both will unfold and accompany the seeker.

Third, commit your ways unto Christ, and he will provide companionship and guidance. He is "the way, the truth, and the life" (John 14:6). He has been "in all points tempted like as we are" (Heb. 5:15), and he will "never leave thee, nor forsake" (Heb. 13:5). Total commitment somehow drives away doubt and replaces it with faith and courage.

Fourth, put your beliefs to the test, put them into action. If they cannot stand the test, they are not worth keeping. Put them to a rigid test, one upon which you can thrust your full weight.

Don't be like the old man who was riding an airplane for the first time, who, when asked how he was enjoying it, said, "I don't know. I haven't yet put all my weight on it."

Faith is not faith until it is tried. Use faith to help you meet the challenge.

Notes

1. From Norman Cox, *Youth's Return to Faith* (Valley Forge, PA.: Judson Press, 1938), p. 19.
2. Caleb Colton, "The New Dictionary of Thought," Tyron Edwards, 1927, p. 141.

10

Through the University of Experience

You are a student, and an apt one I hope, in the university of experience. I suggest that you take more courses, courses that are generally overlooked, yet are most important. The years of experience can teach us what the days know not.

Ben Franklin said, "Experience keeps a dear school; but fools will learn in no other; and scarce in that." Let us try to improve our knowledge from experience because experience can validate reflections, but experiences are not transferable.

Courses to Take

The university of experience has no set curriculum, but I want to suggest four courses for you to take: attitude development, selling yourself, getting along with others, and giving yourself away. These may well provide for you some of the extras needed in whatever course of life you may pursue.

Your *altitude is determined largely by your attitude*. It is important to build a good attitude, to have attitude goals. A popular song of some decades ago went like this, "Accentuate the positive, eliminate the negative . . . have nothing to do with Mr. In-Between." That's good advice.

W. Clement Stone, the highly successful insurance executive, is a great believer in PMA—Positive Mental Attitude. Norman Vincent Peale, noted author, is a great believer in the power of positive thinking. Both Stone and Peale are convinced that a person's attitude truly determines the altitude at which a person lives.

I do not know of a company or a business, except the

newspapers that hire special critics for things like musicals, who are interested in hiring an individual adept at criticizing at all times or one who possesses a vocal, negative attitude. Attitude is the way we look at life. Attitude can grow only through experience. Experiences, though some may be failures, should not defeat us or embitter us. We should try to wring something positive, something helpful, out of each experience. I have had weak, crossed eyes since I was three years old. My parents told me that the measles settled in my eyes and left me cross-eyed. I have had lots of positive fun about my eyes. Glasses will pull them into correct position, but let me take off my glasses and I see two of everything and everyone. When I am speaking to a small audience I frequently remark that we have a good audience, "All I need to do is remove my glasses, and I see two of each one of you . . . a doubling of attendance."

Learn to look, to see, to evaluate all experiences. Do you remember reading about the Philistine giant, Goliath, who frightened the men of Israel? The giant caused terror and fear to possess all but David. Notice the difference in attitude. The Israelites said, "He is so big we cannot overcome him." David said, "He is so big I can't miss him," and David slew Goliath.

Enthusiasm, discipline, vision, faith, and courage will add building blocks to your attitude. Give much personal attention to how you approach each day, each task, and each person. A positive attitude will create a warm climate, a more conducive environment, and a happier disposition. It will be well worth your time and money to buy two or three books on attitude building. Spare neither time nor money in this quest.

Try diligently to sell yourself. Of course, I do not mean that you should sell out to the cheap things of life. Develop instead the art of selling yourself to your employer, your friends, and your larger world of opportunity.

Initially, try to peel away certain barnacles that interfere with your efforts. Dehypnotize yourself; that is, don't be dazed or tranquilized by your own lack of enthusiasm, cheerfulness, and positive mental attitude. Do something to improve. You can, you know! Then "unself" yourself; that is, get rid of that heavy barnacle of ego-centeredness. Don't be a braggart with the malady described as "constipation of ideas and a diarrhea of words." No one gets excited about such a person. Braggadocio is a useless exercise. I fear there are far too many young people like the bold young man who cried out, "I'm for me." "Meism" is likewise a bad malady.

We are all in the business of selling—selling ourselves. It is not an easy task. We know a lot about ourselves, and that is good; for before one can sell, he must know his product. We should try to project the image of a person who is thoughtful of others, dependable, and trustworthy. Our word should be our bond. Personal integrity is important. In order to sell yourself, practice the habit of being alive-eyed with reference to others. Notice little things about your friends. Try to be encouraging and helpful. Give more than is expected of you. Seek opportunities to be of service. Be friendly and courteous. Do not try to cram something down or over someone. Create a desire in others to want to know you better. The tone of one's voice, the gleam in one's eye all contribute to successful selling of self. Two very famous men, unknown to each other, met suddenly. Said one to the other, "Do I know you?"

Said the other, "No, but I wish I knew you."

Little things noticed and remembered in the lives of others frequently create a better climate in the selling of oneself. I had an insurance friend who was trying to sell a prospective buyer a rather large policy. Other salespeople were also in quest of the sale. My friend remembered that the prospective buyer had told him about an injury to his son's hand. The father seemed very concerned, as any father would. On the occasion of the next visit, my friend spent most of the time talking about the son. His personal interest in the son and the man's family, as much as anything else, caused him to be awarded the sales contract. Try to remember birthdays, anniversaries, and other important dates. Try to recall the likes and dislikes of your friends, their eccentricities and idiosyncrasies.

Take a course in the university of experience in *how to handle people* or the art of getting along with others. Sooner or later every one of you who reads this book will be in a place of responsibility. You will become a teacher, plant manager, salesperson, secretary, school superintendent, husband or wife, parent, corporate president, academic dean, or politician. You will soon find out that people don't act as predictably under given circumstances as hydrogen and oxygen. In fact, people are very unpredictable.

A lady went into a shoe store to buy a pair of shoes. The clerk measured her feet and said, "It will be difficult to fit you. One foot is larger than the other." She stormed out of the store, went across the street, and into another shoe shop. Here the clerk said, after measuring her feet, "One foot is smaller than the other, but we can handle that." Happily she purchased the shoes. Note that both clerks in essence said the same thing, only the approach was entirely different.

Being a college president for twenty-three years has caused me to think long and study hard to improve my relationships with others. I have constantly read books and observed the real champions in personnel relations. I have filtered from much reading and observation what I choose to call a "baker's dozen" (13), suggestions to follow in dealing with people in a leadership role or on an equal basis. Here is the "baker's dozen" list:

1. Lead, don't dictate—say at times, "Follow me."
2. Listen. Be available when others want to talk. Don't be an isolationist.
3. Communicate fully, keep the lines open.
4. Delegate responsibility and expect results.
5. Provide additional training.
6. Challenge and inspire your people.
7. Give proper credit to the achievers.
8. Show appreciation and recognition.
9. Show respect and merit respect.

10. Provide adequate recompense and achievement bonuses if possible.
11. Create an atmosphere of job security.
12. Place a premium on pride in good work.
13. Create a good esprit de corps—a good team spirit.

These thirteen suggestions are not a "surefire" method, but I don't know of any organization or individual who has been successful without practicing some or all of these.

In the illustration which follows, notice how many of these principles are operable.

Years ago two boys were working their way through Stanford University. Their funds got desperately low, and the idea came to them to engage Paderewski for a piano recital. They would use the funds to help pay their board and tuition.

The great pianist's manager asked for a guarantee of $2,000, a lot of money in those days; but the boys agreed and promoted the concert, worked hard, but only grossed $1,600. After the concert the two told the great artist the bad news. They gave him the entire $1,600 with a promissory note for $400, explaining they would earn the amount and send it to him. It looked like the end of their college careers.

"No, Boys, that won't do," and tearing the note in two, Paderewski returned the money to them as well. "Now, take out of the $1,600 all of your expenses, keep for each of you 10 percent of the balance for your work. Let me have the rest."

Years passed. World War I came and went. Paderewski, now premier of Poland, was striving to feed the starving people in his native land. He knew of only one man who could help him, Herbert Hoover, who was in charge of the United States Food Relief Bureau. Hoover responded, and thousands of tons of food were sent to Poland.

Later Paderewski journeyed to Paris to thank Hoover for the relief sent. "That's all right, Mr. Paderewski," Hoover replied. "Besides, you don't remember it, but you helped me once when I was a student at college and I was in trouble."

Take a course in *the art of giving yourself away*. Giving is a great spiritual principle which stems from God's giving of himself so abundantly to each of us through the natural and spiritual provisions he has made available. Giving destroys selfishness and creates joy. There is no greater gift than a bit of oneself. Here again God showed us the way by the giving of his Son, Jesus Christ. Miserly people are in most cases very miserable while generous people are usually glad and joyful.

I am deeply indebted to David Dunn for calling my attention so forcibly to this whole matter. I don't know David Dunn personally, but I feel like I know him quite well. He wrote one of the most charming little books I have ever read. The title of it is *Try Giving Yourself Away.* (Buy it now if you can. Read it not once, but several times.) There are 29 chapters in the 106-page book. Here are some of the titles: "Obey your warm-hearted impulses"; "Bread upon the waters"; "Minutes make fine gifts"; "Multiply your giving by three"; "Three-cent [then that was the cost of a postage stamp] giving"; "Little sparks of appreciation"; and "Are you a credit-giver?"[1]

When you stop to think about it, young people are better givers than adults. They don't have much money, so they are better at giving themselves. They have fewer inhibitions and worries about the value of the gift and about whether the gift will please the receiver. They also act impulsively, doing what they think of doing.

I want to tease your mind and tantalize your taste for action by giving you one of the paragraphs from Dunn's book. "In *Your Life,* Marion Simms told the story of a girl who wanted to give her older sister a birthday gift but had no money in the bank. But that didn't stump her. When the sister opened her birthday packages at breakfast, she found an envelope tied with a ribbon. Inside were three colored slips of paper, each with a 'gift' neatly printed on it: 'Good for two dishwashings.' 'Good for three bed makings.' 'Good for two kitchen floor scrubbings.' These three presents were among her most welcome birthday surprises."

Giving becomes habitual. Start to write notes of appreciation to your parents, your teachers, and your friends. Leave them at unusual places, such as on your bed, in your parents' room, on the kitchen table. Select a place to leave one for your teachers. Use the post office to carry a note to a distant friend. Pick up the phone and say something like, "Just wanted you to know I was thinking of you and remembering with gratitude what you did . . . " If you can't think of anything to do or say, look around and observe your friends, your loved ones, and you will soon see things leaping at you.

I have followed the practice each Thanksgiving week to write a thank you note to someone who, during the past twelve months, has done something on my behalf or on behalf of someone else for which I am grateful. This little, rather insignificant practice has produced many rewarding experiences. Just a week ago a lady told me about receiving a note from me twenty-five years ago. Jesus said, "Give, and it shall be given unto you" (Luke 6:38).

Lessons Previously Learned in the University of Experience

I know that the best lesson to be learned is learned by the individual. I know that little is learned from the experience of others, but it is good to share our experiences with each other. Let me, therefore, share with you eight lessons I have learned through life's experiences.

First, I know that there is an ocean because I have seen a babbling brook. "'Where are you going, little brook,' I said, as it pushed along its weary head? 'I'm going to the river, the river to the sea, for that is where all little brooks long to be.'" Brooks run into rivers, and rivers run into the seas. For none of us "liveth to himself, and no man dieth to himself" (Rom. 14:7). No life really achieves its ultimate purpose until it loses itself in the larger sea of humanity serving a cause larger than itself.

Second, I have learned that there are diamonds, for I have seen the sparkling dewdrops. Look out into your front yard some spring morning when the dew is on the grass and when the sun's rays are hitting the dewdrops. You will think your yard is sown with diamonds. I have been at diamond factories in Amsterdam and Haifa, but I brought back no souvenirs. But remember that God doesn't tease us. If the sun upon the dewdrops can make sparkling, glittering images, symbolic of diamonds, we can rest assured that there are some things like that in permanent form. The Bible is full of such sparkling, glittering diamonds. "His name shall be called Wonderful, Counsellor, The Mighty God, The everlasting Father, The Prince of Peace" (Isa. 9:6). "Glory to God in the highest, and on earth peace, good will toward men" (Luke 2:14).

Third, I have learned what faith is because I have planted a garden. It takes faith to grow a garden. It takes faith to put what looks like dead seed into the ground and wait for that seed to sprout and grow. I pushed some seed into the sod and stood back and watched the acts of God. I saw a tiny sprout and soon luxuriant grain and said, "Thank God, a miracle again!" So I know what faith is for it "is the substance of things hoped for, the evidence of things not seen" (Heb. 11:1).

Fourth, I know that there is order and design in the universe because I have peered through a microscope at a tiny, one-cell animal, and I have peered through a telescope at countless stars in the heavens. We may someday vote for a constitutional change of our government, but never will we vote for a constitutional change of the universe. Marvelous and matchless things, both large and small, just didn't happen. A newspaper is not produced by dumping all the type into one big heap and shouting at it to come up with the latest news. Order and design are from God, and thus the universe moves in an orderly fashion.

Fifth, I know that God doesn't speak only English because I have heard many persons of many races, in their native tongues, pray to God. The Bible says that God "hath made of one blood all the nations of men for to dwell on all the face of the earth" (Acts 17:26). God loves everyone. Everyone is precious in the good Lord's sight.

Sixth, I know there is a pot of gold at the end of God's rainbow of promises. As a lad, when I saw a rainbow in the sky, I would frequently call my dog and say to myself, *I am going to find the end of that rainbow and get that pot of gold.* All was well and good until the shadows of darkness would begin to enclose me, then I would return home unsuccessful. How is this for a pot of gold? "Verily, verily, I say unto you, He that believeth on me, the works that I do shall he do also; and greater works than these shall he do; because I go unto my Father" (John 14:12). God's promises are backed by the blood of the Son of God and are more precious than gold.

Seventh, I know what love and forgiveness are because I have been loved and forgiven. Here's an experience I had about twelve years ago.

One morning, as I walked off the front of Blanton Hall, I said, "Good morning, Jim" to a young man that I never saw again. One Sunday after the evening service at the church where his father was minister of music, Jim took his girl friend to a hamburger place and then on to her home. Returning to his home, he came to an intersection with a traffic light which had turned green. He started through the intersection only to have his car rammed by a car driven by a young man under the influence of alcohol who had come to the city on a football scholarship. The drunken driver was trying to elude the police. Jim was knocked sixty feet out of his car. He was taken to the hospital. For four hours doctors sought to remove glass from his skull and brain. They told his mother and father, "He won't live very long."

On Thursday the doctor told Jim's mother and father, "The minutes are few." The mother asked the young man who had caused the accident, his parents, and her pastor to go with her to the prayer chapel at the hospital. She directed her pastor to sit with the young man's parents on one side of the chapel. She took the young man to the other side of the chapel.

Sitting down she took his hand in her hands and said, "My son, Jim, loved athletics. You'll have to play for two now because he's practically gone. My son never touched alcohol; he wishes you would never touch it again, seeing what has happened. My son, Jim, was a good student, and he would like for you to give priorities where priorities are due. My son, Jim, was a Christian." Then mustering all the forgiveness and love a brokenhearted mother could muster, she said, "Because Jim was a Christian, Jim would forgive you; I forgive you." I know what love and forgiveness are when I experience it like that.

Eighth, I know there is a hereafter because of what we are after here—peace, love, and joy—but they escape us here. We are after perfection and an absence of pain and suffering, but those things don't leave us alone here. But God has promised us a life in the hereafter where there is complete joy, peace, and love with no pain or suffering. I know there is a hereafter because God never fails, and his Son has gone to prepare that place for us.

These are the lessons I have learned, and I hope you will have the joy of learning them or some like them for yourself.

Ways to Handle Experiences Learned

Experiences learned in the university of experience can be costly. The tuition you will pay varies because you will determine that cost by how quickly you learn and how carefully you handle your courses. This university majors also on continuing education, some courses running for a lifetime.

Catalog your mistakes and failures, and learn from your library of mistakes. Mistakes and failures are not all bad. A child learns to walk by trying, by falling down and trying again. When I was twelve years old, I was given a pair of ice skates for Christmas. I could hardly wait until a hard freeze came, making the ice on the pond thick and safe enough to try out my skates. I went out midmorning and continued until midafternoon. I don't remember how many times I fell on the ice; but by the time I stopped for the day, I could skate. I could stand up and glide slowly across the pond. Certainly, I was not and am not an accomplished skater, but I can still skate. I have not forgotten how to skate: only now my fear of falling is greater.

Even though mistakes come, stay active in the arena and don't try to escape involvement. I have told students that if and when they fail, I much prefer that their failure be due to attempting to do something rather than sitting down and doing nothing. Tackle the difficult. Hack away at the seemingly impossible. All things in time will yield.

Note

1. David Dunn, *Try Giving Yourself Away* (Englewood Cliffs, NJ.: Prentice Hall, 1956).

11

Through the Marketplace Toward the Land of Beginning Again

Through the Marketplace

The term *marketplace* is being used here to denote the place where you will spend your energy either preparing for your life's work or the energy you will spend in your life's work. Wherever you now find yourself is a place that in some respects is cruel, complex, highly competitive, impersonal, and uncertain.

A high school diploma is no assurance that your college work will be successful. A college diploma is no assurance that you will find a good job and succeed in it as you enter the larger marketplace of the business world. You will find it hard to earn a living, hard to gain promotions, and hard to come out on top in your work, but you *can* achieve all of these things.

Always give 212° effort, not 211°. At 211° water is just hot water, maybe too hot to touch, but inert and incapable of much power. Add that extra degree ($211° + 1° = 212°$), and water becomes live steam, and you know what steam can do: pull a locomotive, heat a building, or if it is under too great a pressure, it can blow up sizable objects. One degree is a small percentage of 212°, but without that last degree the previous 211° are powerless.

Strive to make things happen. It is said that everywhere he went Jesus either created a riot or a revolution. A car in neutral won't climb many hills. Inertia doesn't solve many problems. Ambition, enthusiasm, hard work, and honesty are good catalysts to start something boiling. Now, please don't infer that I am suggesting that you should be a troublemaker by always stirring up the water. What I am saying is that there is a gift of God within each person that should be stirred into motion, and when that occurs things will happen. Lethargy and indolence are not high on the value scale of the achiever. Try to create a market for your talents.

During my school days when we would choose sides to play either basketball or softball, I never wanted to be the last person chosen. The first person chosen was usually the most talented player. You can be the first person chosen in your classroom, in your dormitory, in your club or fraternity, and out in the marketplace if you will always strive to keep your talents, abilities, and commitments at 212°.

In trying to stay at 212°, remember that you may fall, but it isn't *how hard you fall but how high you bounce.* When you fall flat on your face get up quickly and stand tall. A defeat or a setback should not produce total disaster but should provide a learning experience to remember. Life has much resiliency.

On a golf course years ago on the outskirts of Atlanta a crowd was watching a man putt time and again eighteen inches from the cup. The man was recognized as the great golfer, Bobby Jones. He was practicing an eighteen-inch putt a thousand times because he had missed an eighteen-inch putt in a tournament a few days previously. He was determined that such would not happen to him again. His intention was to bounce back, higher than before.

Stumbling blocks can be changed to stepping-stones if we would only learn from the fall and take the next step with greater skill, confidence, and assurance. We should be quick to shake off the dust from our fall and go onward and upward.

The pathway to success is not a comfortable bed nor a soft path without stones or sharp turns. A's in the classroom are not automatic, nor are promotions in the marketplace automatic. Both come by diligent application of the resources at hand.

Don't get upset with yourself or others when you have tried and failed. Blind rage, being "mad as a wet hen," and "fit to be tied" work against rather than for the individual. "The best time to tell what makes one tick is when he is all wound up."

Getting uptight and upset easily calls for a good look at why such is occurring. A temperamental person may be described as one displaying 90 percent temper and 10 percent mental. It is generally true that persons stumble over pebbles, never over mountains. Seneca said, "The greatest remedy for anger is delay." Simply experiencing a moment of anger rather than acting it out may prevent a day of sorrow. I ask you, What is your upset size? Watch the speed and frequency of your wrath.

We all get upset. We are not perfect.

When hatred of and resentment toward others take hold, try practicing the art of "Love your enemies" (Matt. 5:44). In so many cases, a soft answer will turn away wrath. Speak slowly and speak softly.

An employer became so angry at an employee in a personal confrontation that he fell dead with a heart attack. Health books talk about ulcer patients whose active ulcers would heal when the victim removed the long-standing resentment and jealousies and replaced them with love and kindness.

A Chinese proverb says, "The fire you kindle for your enemy often burns yourself more than him."

"He that is slow to anger is better than the mighty; and he that ruleth his spirit than he that taketh a city" (Prov. 16:32).

In the crowded marketplace of life, whether on campus or in the busy world of employment, *self-discipline is vital to success.* There are times when we just must make ourselves do things whether we like them or not. In the process of self-discipline, strive to do your best by forcing yourself to do those things that are proven as worthy and appropriate.

Your inner consciousness may tell you that you should cut down on smoking, or quit it altogether, but in all likelihood you will do nothing about it until your doctor tells you of the harm you are doing to your body. Or you are goofing off in the classroom. You know that exam time is coming soon and that your written assignment is not on target, but you continue to put off everything, hoping to catch up at the last minute. But you don't; then it is too late.

Here is a good exercise to do: Sit in a chair facing another chair. Imagine yourself in the other chair. Take a solid look at the person in the second chair. What do you see? Do you like what you see? Then imagine that your many selves are seated around a table in a meeting. As presiding officer, take a vote as to which self will preside over the board and then discipline yourself accordingly. I hope the group of selves would elect your highest and best self instead of the selfish self or the passionate self or the careless self or the miserly self.

A traveler in ancient Greece lost his way. In desperation he asked a man standing on the roadside, who happened to be the venerable Socrates, how to get to Mount Olympus. The sage replied, "Just make every step you take go in that direction." There is much wisdom and good advice in such a reply. Going off on every tangent and chasing every whim or passing fancy won't lead to upper levels.

General Robert E. Lee told his men, and I am sure he said it also to his students at Washington College, "I cannot consent to place in the control of others one who cannot control himself." Discipline should be an ally, clung to tenaciously, rather than an enemy. There is nothing wrong with periodically, if not daily, calling oneself into account by asking such questions as, What have I overcome today? What temptation have I resisted? What virtue have I gained? How have I done that which I ought to have done?

One of the secrets of self-discipline is the control of one's thoughts. Thought actions give birth to and control most all other actions. Another secret of self-control is the practice of reason. When these two are carefully followed, there still comes a time when one must stand straight and utter the words *No* and *No, thank you.* You and I are free, thank God, to say No.

If you go into the arena of life, whether at school or at work, with a desire to challenge and to lead, then have a compass in your head and a magnet in your heart. No one can lead others without knowing where to go and how to get there.

You will find along your way that life has four windows: east, south, north, and west.

Through the *eastern window* of life can be seen the rising sun. You will thrill with the breaking of a new day. Happily and gratefully in God's plan when the day breaks it brings opportunities for service and love, an occasion of joy. Welcome, always, the dawn.

Peering through life's *southern window* you will find the heat from the toils and the tasks of the day providing a warmth and glow of satisfaction if the job is done well. The southern window ripens the fruit of your labors.

The *northern window* brings in the north wind and gives you a glimpse of the storms of life. Some days will be dark and dreary and turbulent. There is a seeming paradox about the northern window; even though the cold winds and storms of life come that way, the artists who give us the beautiful paintings that enrich our museums, galleries, and homes paint in a room with windows facing the north in order to get the truest colors. This is symbolic of the beautiful things of life coming frequently from the storms and struggles of life.

Lastly, go to the *western window* and view the setting sun, as the shadows of the day bring on darkness. The color of the rays of the sun splashed on the western sky provide a good background for self-evaluation and inventory of the day's activities. Has the day gone well? Has some worthy action been done? Has a friend been helped? Have I moved closer to my goal in life? Have I disciplined myself in matters of importance?

The windows of life never close until we depart for the land of beginning again where there is no need of the sun, the moon, and the stars.

To the Land of Beginning Again

Louisa Fletcher Tarkington wrote a beautiful poem entitled "The Land of Beginning Again." In that poem she expressed a wish, which I have had many times, that there was some wonderful place where we could begin all over.

I wish that there were some wonderful place
Called the Land of Beginning Again,

Where all our mistakes and all our heartaches
And all of our poor, selfish grief
Could be dropped, like a shabby old coat, at the door,
   And never be put on again.

I wish we could come on it all unaware,
   Like the hunter who finds a lost trail;
And I wish that the one whom our blindness had done
The greatest injustice of all
Could be at the gates, like an old friend that waits
   For the comrade he's gladdest to hail.

We would find all the things we intended to do
   But forgot, and remembered too late,
Little praises unspoken, little promises broken,
And all of the thousand and one
Little duties neglected that might have perfected
   The day for one less fortunate.

It wouldn't be possible not to be kind
   In the Land of Beginning Again;
And the ones we misjudged and the ones whom we grudged
Their moments of victory here,
Would find in the grasp of our loving handclasp
   More than penitent lips could explain.

For what had been hardest we'd know had been best,
   And what had seemed lost would be gain;
For there isn't a sting that will not take wing
When we've faced it and laughed it away;
And I think that the laughter is most what we're after
   In the Land of Beginning Again!

So I wish that there were some wonderful place
   Called the Land of Beginning Again,
Where all our mistakes and all our heartaches
And all of our poor selfish grief,
Could be dropped, like a shabby old coat, at the door,
   And never be put on again.[1]

There is no doubt but that in the land of beginning again some of the things that had been lost would be regained. The poem is idealistic, and yet it is realistic.

Each day is a land of beginning again because the heartaches, mistakes, poor judgments, grudges, and unkept promises of the previous day need not be picked up.

Each new job is the land of beginning again. Each new assignment is the land of beginning again, just as is each new course taken and each new semester begun. We are not imprisoned in an iron cage with every hour and every day the same.

Two personalities from the Bible show dramatically what it is to move into the land of beginning again.

Naaman was a captain of the host of the king of Syria (2 Kings 5). He was a man of valour, *but* he had leprosy, a terrible disease of that day, considered incurable. Naaman's wife was told by her maid of a prophet of God in Samaria who could heal Naaman. Naaman went to the king of Israel. The prophet Elisha heard about the meeting between the king and Naaman. The prophet asked that Naaman come to him. Upon arriving at the prophet's house, Naaman was told to wash in the Jordan River seven times. This seemed to be an absurd cure to Naaman, and he was mad. He thought little of the river Jordan in comparison to the Abana and Pharpar rivers of Damascus. But his servants pleaded with him to do what the prophet had said. Upon doing just that, he found that his flesh became like the flesh of a little child. He was cured physically and moved from the land of leprosy into the land of beginning again. It was a new life for him.

Saul, a brilliant student of Gamaliel and the Jewish law, was breathing out threats of prison and slaughter against the followers of Christ. However, on his way to Damascus, a bright light encompassed him, and he heard a voice saying, "Saul, Saul, why persecutest thou me?" (Acts 9:4). In response, Saul was taken to Damascus to the home of Judas (v. 11), and while there God sent Ananias to him. God called Saul to "bear my name before the Gentiles" (v. 15). Saul (Paul) then entered into the spiritual land of beginning again. He found the experiences tough, painful, and frightening but rewarding in the long run.

There is one great land of beginning again where all things are even beyond our greatest imagination. That land or place is heaven. It is being prepared for us by Christ himself. He said he was going to do just that, but he expects us to be preparing ourselves for what he is preparing for us.

Preparation for that wonderful place is made by living in accordance with the commandments laid down in the Bible. Sin and corruption cannot inherit life everlasting. We should work harder preparing for heaven than we work preparing to live. We will spend eternity there. We do not know when our number will come up, but:

> Some day the bell will sound,
> Some day my heart will bound,
> As with a shout,
> That school is out,
> And, lessons done,
> I homeward run.
> —Maltbie Babcock

If you are not already excited about going to heaven when you die, let me tell you a bit about heaven with the hope that you will anticipate it with such excitement that you will begin today to make adequate preparation.

Heaven is described in the Bible as the eternal home of those who have accepted Christ as their Savior, Lord, and Master. Heaven's gate cannot be crashed. There is only one entrance gate, and that is by grace through faith. Heaven is a place for weary feet, a place of joy and rest. Heaven is a mansion for the poor, wayfaring pilgrim. It is for the longing soul the gift of satisfaction. It is for the sinful, dying thief the gift of paradise.

Even though Jesus is there preparing a place for us, we must send ahead those things from which he constructs our place. Unless we send our cleansed hearts thither, we will not get there. Unless we lay up for ourselves treasures in heaven, there will be no treasures for us. The beautiful thing is that Christ takes and magnifies what we have sent ahead, and the beauty of his work is beyond our imagination.

We can't talk our way into heaven by sounding pious and sweet. Heaven is truly the land of beginning again only after we have confessed our sins to Christ, accepted through faith his redeeming grace, and acknowledged him as Savior, Lord, and Master. He holds the key to heaven's gate. You will do well to grasp the unseen hand when your little boat is severely tossed to and fro.

Note

1. Louisa Fletcher Tarkington, "The Land of Beginning Again" in Frederick F. Shannon, *The Land of Beginning Again* (Old Tappan, N.J.: Fleming H. Revell Company, 1921), pp. 7-8.

Section IV
How Do I Get There?

Thus far in *Meeting the Challenges,* we have asked three basic questions: Who are you? Why are you here? and Where do you go from here?

The fourth major question is: How do I get there?

There is no better map available than one drawn by Henry Van Dyke in his poem entitled *Four Things*:

> Four things a man must learn to do
> If he would make his record true:
> To think without confusion clearly;
> To love his fellowmen sincerely;
> To act from honest motives purely;
> To trust in God and Heaven securely.

Regardless of the amount of thought and attention given to the three previous major questions, little will be accomplished unless there is diligent pursuit of the right course. There must be a destination in the journey through life. There is an old saying "All roads lead to Rome," but all roads do not lead to the land of achievement and acceptable stewardship. In taking a trip, it is far better to map out the course of travel in advance rather than going haphazardly.

12

To Think
Without Confusion Clearly

Don't let anyone tell you that it is easy to think clearly. Emerson remarked that the hardest task a person has is to think. Thoughts can generate health and energy or put toxins in the system. The Bible says, and philosophers and thinkers of all kinds agree, that as a person thinks so is he (Prov. 23:7). Truly our minds are our kingdoms.

There is no set formula for thinking clearly. The need, however, for such thinking has never been greater than it is today. Individuals can't agree, experts can't agree, governments and nations are in confusion. There is widespread confusion.

This chapter asks two questions: Are you a victim of "stinkin' thinkin'"? and Do you have "psychosclerosis"? After dealing with those questions, I make three very strong, positive suggestions: wear your thinking cap daily, try to possess a divine insanity of the mind, and think and be thankful.

Are You a Victim of "Stinkin' Thinkin'"?

The words used in that question may not be too sophisticated, but the point is there. Stinkin' thinkin' comes from habitual harboring of prejudices about persons, traditions, and religion to name only a few.

Some little daily event or episode can easily prejudice minds and harm efforts at clear thinking. This can occur in the classroom or in the home or in the marketplace. Have you ever had a teacher who made some remark about an assignment or an event that did not set well with you, and immediately your

133

thinking became stinkin' thinkin' because you made up your mind right there and then not to change your mind nor to approach the assignment or problem with an open mind? Your thoughts began to decay and putrefy. Has someone in your family ever said something that prejudiced your actions and decisions to the extent that you closed your mind to any further consideration of the total picture? Your thoughts in that respect became stinkin' thinkin'.

Have you ever said to yourself, *I don't like that person, and I never will*? Think back as to what made you think that way. Was your pride hurt? Was an unkind or inaccurate remark made about you? Did that person perform better than you, causing jealousy? Or did you make a snap judgment about that person, basing your judgment on an initial impression?

It is quite easy in religious matters to become so straitlaced as to look upon those who do not agree with you as less religious than you. We tend to judge our religious friends by a rule other than the Golden Rule. We usually expect others to do more than we do and to act more lovingly and forgivingly while on the other hand we think of ourselves as better than they.

On the international scene it is very easy to practice stinkin' thinkin'! I have heard people refer to the Japanese as "Japs" and to Italians as "Wops" and "Dagos." We are guilty of allowing incidents by nations to prejudice us toward everyone of those nationalities.

Prejudices may be more harmful to us than someone else's prejudice toward us. It is good to keep an open mind and to try very hard to approach things objectively and persistently.

A wise and prudent young person will watch very carefully what goes into the mind. Dirty jokes, off-color stories, the content of trashy books, and obscene movie scenes when allowed to occupy the mind are as detrimental to the mind as drinking water from a polluted lake, eating unwashed fruit, and breathing impure air are detrimental to the body. Stinkin' thinkin' is very hard to control. Give it as much attention at least as you give to your teeth and breath.

Do You Have "Psychosclerosis"?

You may not find the word *psychosclerosis* in the dictionary, but it is a very descriptive word meaning "the hardening of the mind," like *arteriosclerosis* means "the hardening of the arteries." Dr. Norman Vincent Peale may have coined this word in one of his books, I am not sure.

Hardening of the arteries is a disease primarily of old age. The hardening of the mind seems to strike youth almost as frequently as it strikes any other age group.

Young people are easy victims for a quick mind-set, or hardening of the mind. You are emerging as thinkers and feel it imperative to express opinions. You are quick to jump on another's mental bandwagon. I have heard young people say time and again, "Oh well, it's another rainy day." Maybe rain does interfere with an outside activity, but it nourishes the earth and cleanses the air. And we appreciate sunny days all the more after a few rainy days.

How many times have you said or heard someone say, "Today is Blue Monday?" None needs to fall in line with that kind of thinking by calling Monday "Blue Monday" and infering that somehow we would like to escape Monday and go on to Tuesday. May I ask what is blue about Monday? I think it is a blue-ribbon day. It is the day after Sunday, which is a day of rest and worship. Monday is the beginning of another week of work and study. Fortunately, Tuesday comes after Monday, and Monday comes after Sunday. The order is great, and we can make each day a great day.

Another tendency of youth comes through expressions like: "Parents just don't understand. They don't know what the situation is. They are not 'with it,' too far removed from what young people like and dislike. They are too old to have viable opinions." Expressions like those are not from young persons who think clearly. A dogmatic mind frequently stems from an insecure mind. A young adult once remarked, "When I was sixteen I was amazed at how little my parents knew; but when I became twenty-two, I was amazed at how much I thought they had learned over that six-year period."

As a youngster I told my mother that I didn't like gooseberry pie. I thought it was too sour. One day she baked a gooseberry pie and put some red coloring in it. I went to the table and thought it was cherry pie and after eating the first piece asked for a second one. At that point my mother said, "Herbert, you know, don't you, that the pie is gooseberry pie?" I didn't eat the second piece. Why? I had a bad case of psychosclerosis. Interestingly enough, I now like gooseberry pie.

Have you ever said to yourself, *I don't care what my parents think, I don't care what my teachers think, I am going to do it anyway?* I hope you have never had such a bad case of psychosclerosis. Such stubbornness is not a part of wisdom. You would do well to think twice, even three times, before doing something contrary to the opinion of your parents and teachers. They just might be right.

Wear Your Thinking Cap Daily

Put on your thinking cap when you first awaken and wear it throughout the day and night. Think in the morning, think at noon, think all day long. Don't be caught without your thinking cap on.

Whenever confronted with a decision involving what is right and what is wrong, try these approaches to finding an answer. Think it through. Use good judgment, common sense, and rational evaluation. Recall the Golden Rule, and play the game by doing unto others as you would have others do unto you (Matt. 7:12; Luke 6:31). Be a good sport. Try never to act less than your best. Play your best. Ask yourself these questions: Am I following the generally accepted moral and ethical standards of society? Am I in line with the teachings of the Ten Commandments and the Sermon on the Mount? Run your intended decision by someone whom you respect and admire greatly. Get another opinion. Always take the long look by asking, Where will this action bring me: to a higher plateau or to a dark valley or a pen of swine?

The Bible is very helpful here. "Whatsoever ye do, do all to the glory of God" (1 Cor. 10:31). Say therefore to yourself, *I will not engage in any form of activity or recreation that will bring reproach upon Christ or dishonor to his name.*

Know ye not that . . . "ye are not your own? For ye are bought with a price: therefore glorify God in your body" (1 Cor. 6:19-20). Therefore, *I will keep my body clean and healthy. I will make it a fit dwelling for the Holy Spirit.*

"I will eat no flesh while the world standeth, lest I make my brother to offend" (1 Cor. 8:13). I will affirm this: *I will not engage in any amusement that will cause a weaker friend to question or doubt or probably stumble.*

"The wages of sin is death" (Rom. 6:23). *I will not engage in activity that will bring eternal regret to me, my parents, my friends, or my school.*

Have you ever given any thought as to what harm, if any, there might be in such popular things as video games and rock music? Does it come as a surprise to you to know that recently *The Tennessean,* published in Nashville (Nov. 10, 1982), carried an article stating that the United States Surgeon General, C. Everrett Coop, said video games may be hazardous to the health of young people by creating adverse mental and physical effects? "There is nothing constructive in the games," he said, especially those that project enemies that have to be killed, for "everything is eliminate, kill, destroy, and let's get up and do it fast." These games coupled with television can tend to make us ready to accept real violence but hopefully not mimic it.

Or let us take the case of rock music. Have you ever thought about it having the possibility of being harmful? In the September 1982 publication of *Moody* magazine, there is an article under the caption "Rock Music—Stairway to Heaven or Highway to Hell?" The article points out that "satanic messages are hidden in some music through backward masking. Album covers picture occult symbols, and rock artists promote promiscuity and perversions." Many songs in contemporary popular music depict hard-drinking men, drugs, husbands with others' wives, each cheating on the other, divorce, and one-night stands. Think about these things. Look for yourself. You be the judge. Keep your thinking cap on all day long.

Develop a Divine Insanity of the Mind

Does that sound paradoxical to you? What is meant by "divine insanity of the mind"?

I think the best way to try to understand what is meant by "divine insanity" is to look at four individuals who were possessed with that trait. The first two are biblical persons, and the other two were outstanding Americans.

Daniel, who lived in Jerusalem around 600 BC, was captured by King Nebuchadnezzar's army and taken with the first exiles to Babylon. In Babylon Daniel distinguished himself by refusing to eat "the portion of the king's meat, nor the wine which he drank" (Dan. 1:8). There is no doubt but that Daniel was thinking clearly and that it was a divine insanity of a noble mind. The temptations were great, but Daniel's conviction was greater. In making the decision about food when he was young and years later when he was in the lion's den, God was with Daniel.

The apostle *Paul,* in writing to the Christians at Galatia, said, "God forbid that I should glory, save in the cross of our Lord Jesus Christ, by whom the world is crucified unto me, and I unto the world" (Gal. 6:14). A statement of that sort indicates a total resignation of self to the wishes of God and the glory of Christ. It places the mind in service to the high and noble things of the spiritual world—a divine insanity of noble minds. Paul lived up to that noble commitment.

On May 20, 1927, *Charles A. Lindbergh* took off from New York City in his airplane, *The Spirit of St. Louis,* attempting to make the first solo flight across the Atlantic Ocean. Thirty-three and one-half hours after takeoff, his plane touched down near Paris. He had succeeded, aided by that divine insanity of a noble mind. Years later he joined with a well-known scientist, Alexis Carrell, to develop an "artificial heart." Lindbergh gave the world an example of courage, stamina, mental acumen, and physical skill.

Born January 15, 1929, the son of a Baptist minister, *Martin Luther King, Jr.*, rose to nationwide fame in 1956 when he was in charge of the city-wide boycott of Montgomery, Alabama's public transportation facilities by Blacks reacting against racial discrimination. He reached the pinnacle of his public acclaim with his Washington, DC, address on August 28, 1963, when he delivered his never-to-be-forgotten speech, "I Have a Dream." He won the Nobel Peace Prize in 1964. He contributed greatly to the enactment of 1964 and 1965 Civil Rights Acts. He was shot in Memphis, Tennessee, on April 4, 1968. King once said, "Every man should have something he would be willing to die for. A man who won't die for something is not really fit to live." He was possessed with a divine insanity of a noble mind.

A person possessed with that divine insanity of a noble mind has a mind and heart totally committed to truth, the highest values, unselfishness, courage, and service to God and humanity.

Think and Be Thankful

Thinking clearly normally leads one to a spirit of thankfulness. It is easy to conclude that we are guests on earth and not proprietors. God is the proprietor. The earth and the heavens have been good to us. The sun, the rain, the soil, and the freedom to work are all blessings for which a thoughtful person will be thankful.

Our ancestors placed on the calendar a Thanksgiving Day for recalling our blessings. There is no day on the calendar for focusing on honesty, integrity, how to make money, or how to be happy. Gratitude then is more important and a vital part of our recognition of the sovereignty of God.

Gratitude for blessings received and for opportunities available will produce in one a very positive attitude in meeting the challenges. God's presence in the past and the assurance of his continued presence enhances faith.

As I think of the challenges I have met and of the challenges you are meeting, I would like to give you three Scripture verses to hold on to as you meet the challenges.

"For God hath not given us the spirit of fear; but of power, and of love, and of a sound mind" (2 Tim. 1:7).

"I can do all things through Christ which strengtheneth me" (Phil. 4:13).

"My God shall supply all your need according to his riches in glory by Christ Jesus" (Phil. 4:9).

Let your heart and mind cling tenaciously to these verses. Be grateful for all things, for thanksgiving is "thanksliving." It costs nothing to be grateful. Try to say thank you more and more and really mean it. I dare you!

Remember, a clear mind will help bring about strength to meet the challenge.

13

To Love Others Sincerely

If one were to write a speech using the subject "To Love Your Fellowman Sincerely," the subject would lend itself immediately to three points: to love, your fellowman, and sincerely. I can do no better than that and shall arrange my thoughts thusly.

It is difficult to cast the meaning of "to love" in the right context. The modern usage is normally way out of line. We hear frequently statements like: "I love football, tennis, and basketball." "I love steak, medium rare, if you please." "I love my Fiat and Honda." "I love computer science, but I hate courses in literature." In each case, the use of the word *love* is inappropriate. One cannot love that which cannot return that love. We may like sports, certain foods, this car over that car, or one course of study better than another; but we do not love those things, for they cannot return our love. We like those things.

Love is a deep word. God is love, and love for others should come from God's love of every person. Love is not based on the weather. Love continues through both fair weather and foul weather. An ardent young lover, in trying to impress his sweetheart, wrote, "Dear, I love you so much I could climb the highest mountain for a glimpse of you. I could swim the widest ocean for one look at your lovely face. I would be willing to spend my last dollar just to see your darling smile. I will be there tonight if it doesn't rain." What shallow nonsense. No real love is conditioned by the weather.

To love others is more difficult, especially when we are to love all persons. Some people are more attractive than others. Some are just easier to love than others. But as members of the human race, created in the image of God, we have no other option if we would be truly Christian because all are brothers and sisters.

In 1949 I was with a party in Rome, Italy, visiting a small Baptist church. As we were seated in the auditorium of the church, my eyes were taking in the writing in Latin of the Lord's Prayer on the walls when suddenly I perked up. "Where have I seen you people before?" the minister asked. "You look very familiar. Have you been here before?" I muttered to myself a subdued no. Others shook their heads in the negative.

The minister added, "Well, I have been to the United States one time. You all are from there I see. But I don't remember seeing you there." Then he really drove home his point, "You see," he said, "we are all Christians, brothers and sisters in Christ; and brothers and sisters just have a way of looking alike." He, too, was 100 percent right.

We have a great opportunity to show that love for people. A Thanksgiving speaker this year said that there are over 650,000,000 people who are dying from hunger. I wonder if an amount almost equal to that number did not feel stuffed from overindulging. The needs of the world, coming from our brothers and sisters, are crying out day and night.

Love wants to share. Love is generous. Real love will find a way to do something about the hunger and hurt in our world. We need desperately to recognize our common obligation.

To love others sincerely is very difficult. *Sincerely* is a strong word in its meaning. It comes from two Latin words, *sine* and *cerus*, meaning "without wax." It was a term used to describe a piece of furniture that was genuinely solid, free of holes filled with plastic wood and waxed over. To love sincerely means to love without sham or pretense; to love truthfully, honestly and without deceit. Sincere love is love that has counted the cost, love that is willing to endure all things, love that is not easily provoked, but is willing to bear all things, believe all things, hope all things, and endure all things (1 Cor. 13:5-7).

In the fall of 1930 I went to Russellville, Kentucky, to enter Bethel Junior College. I had $40.00 which I had borrowed from my sister, a school teacher. Those were the Depression years. After five weeks (imagine $40.00 lasting five weeks in college), all of my money was gone. I had no choice but to pack and head back to the little farm owned by my father. Packing was an easy chore since I had only one suitcase for my belongings—no radio, TV, or stereo—and very few clothes. I went to the dining hall the evening before going home and ate at the table with my English teacher. We talked of many things, and I got around to telling her that I would no longer be in her classes because I was leaving the next morning. I arose to leave the table, asked to be excused, but Miss Yancey said, "Herbert, wait for me in the hallway. I want to see you." I wondered why she wanted to see me. I waited what seemed like an eternity. Had I split an infinitive; had I butchered the king's English?

Finally, she came out of the dining room. I was waiting nervously. She said, "Herbert, I don't want you to leave. I want you to stay in school."

My reply to her was, "Miss Yancey, I must go home, for I have no money."

"If you will stay, I will help you," she said. I couldn't believe my ears. "You stay, and I will help you."

I don't know why I said what I did. I quiveringly responded, "Miss Yancey, I do appreciate what you have said, but I couldn't accept money from a woman your age." Imagine a freshman saying that to his English teacher, but I did. I was trying to be nice. I knew the college was having a hard time and probably not paying the faculty full salary. She had some white hair and I, as a lad just turned sixteen, thought that anyone with white hair had one foot in the grave.

"Oh, you are nice, but I want to help you."

"Well, all right, I will stay if you help me get a job."

"I will go tomorrow and speak to the president," she said.

She did speak to the president, and I stayed, raking leaves, firing furnaces, and cleaning out rest rooms. Would you believe that at the end of the semester the college owed me thirty-five cents, and I was richer at that time than at any time since.

About twelve years ago I took my wife and our three daughters to Mays Lick, Kentucky, to visit with Miss Yancey. I wanted her to meet our family, and most of all I wanted to thank her sincerely for loving me sincerely. I had maintained correspondence with her through the years, but this trip was special to me. My last letter from her was shortly before her death at ninety-nine years of age. She apologized for her writing because the lines were not straight. She wrote, "And now, as I near the end of the way, one thought keeps coming to me 'Must I go, and empty-handed, Thus my dear Redeemer meet.'" I wrote her the day after receiving her letter to say, "Miss Yancey, many of us will go empty-handed, but not you. As long as I live you will live through me, and no doubt my coming to the presidency of Belmont College was influenced by your assistance to me as a freshman. I want to help students as you helped me." She was one person, other than my family, who taught me what it means to love others sincerely.

The world is hungry for love. It needs a lot of loving. Fortunately, you and I can give it a lot of loving. If we will only think of people as our brothers and sisters, then we will give them our love. If we will look for the good in each person, we will no doubt find some good in each one. If we will strive to love and appreciate each one, we are likely to find that we will be more loved and appreciated.

It has always been of interest to me to see how little people like to carry their baby brothers or sisters, who are almost as heavy as themselves. I feel the basic reason behind such action was expressed when an onlooker asked, "Sonny, isn't the brother you are carrying awfully heavy?"

"Oh, no Sir, you see, he's my brother. He ain't heavy." And it does make a world of difference.

No campus, society, or world can be sturdily built on hate. The only foundation that will stand is one of love. If we would be willing to pool our energies, our resources, our talents and our love, we could build on love.

The thirteenth chapter of 1 Corinthians, called the love

chapter, gives one of the most beautiful descriptions of love ever penned by human hands. I believe very sincerely there is enough truth in that chapter to change the world if only the world would practice it.

I have referred previously in this book to Tennyson. Would you consider it unusual for a poet of his acclaim who wrote so many poems to say that his greatest stanza was one from "Locksley Hall":

> Love took up the harp of life, and smote
>   on all the chords with might;
> Smote the chord of self, that, trembling,
>   passed in music out of sight.

Tennyson truly knew the value of love. Do we?

14

To Act from
Honest Motives Purely

It is tough, very tough, to act always from honest motives. The unregenerate heart is "deceitful above all things, and desperately wicked: who can know it?" (Jer. 17:9), and no heart is pure unless both the motives and the actions are pure. Most persons are more than likely to attempt at times to negotiate with their motives since motives are invisible and out of sight of the onlooker. No one, therefore, is able to detect any weakness, but God reads unerringly all motives and motives are the expressions of the soul.

Piousity is no substitute or cover-up for impure motives. Acting the part of the good guy and sounding like a "chanting monk" are not equal to acting from honest motives. The motive may be good at times while the action is impure.

An after-Christmas edition of our college paper, *The Vision*, ran an article on the subject, "What Did You Do During the Holidays?" One of the male students told of going into Founders Hall, an old dormitory no longer in use, taking a bentwood rocker, refinishing it, and giving it to his minister of music. When I read the account I called the student to my office. To protect anonymity I shall refer to him as Jack.

"Jack," I asked after passing some pleasantries, "Did *The Vision* accurately report your Christmas activities?"

"Yes, Sir," he replied.

"May I ask you a question? Who owned that rocker which you took from Founders Hall?"

Sheepishly he asked, "Are you going to say what I think you are?"

147

"Yes. I imagine that you are thinking the same thing I am thinking. That rocker didn't belong to you; it belonged to the college."

"Yes, I was thinking that and wonder why I didn't think about it when I took the rocker."

"Jack, you give me $7.50 right now for that rocker which I will turn into the finance office. You are a premed student, aren't you? Don't ever take such liberties with your patients. Think long and hard."

He gave me the money and thanked me most profusely, and his dad called from another city to thank me. Today that young man is an honest, upstanding doctor.

His action was rather commonplace. People think that if something is not in use it may be taken. Motel towels and other supplies seem to fall into the same category.

Expediency or need doesn't make a thing right for the doer if the deed is innately wrong. It is wrong to see how far the truth can be stretched or how white a lie can be made. A lie is a lie.

Our nation has honored the memory of one of its presidents by constantly referring to him as "Honest Abe." Abraham Lincoln got that name from his actions as a clerk in Offutt's store at New Salem. One day he sold a lady a little bale of goods amounting to, by his reckoning, $2.20. He rechecked his figures after the purchaser left and found that he had made a six cent error. At night, after the closing of the store, he walked two to three miles to deliver the six cents. On another occasion, at the close of the day, a woman asked for eight ounces of tea. He weighed the tea, but upon entering the store the next morning he noticed that there was a four-ounce weight instead of an eight-ounce weight on the scales. Realizing his mistake, he closed the store and walked a great distance to deliver the tea before breakfast. In both cases, he acted from honest motives but made a mistake and set about immediately to correct the errors.

A minister friend of mine, who rode a city bus, was given twenty-five cents too much in change. He noticed the error only upon taking his seat. As he left the bus, he handed the quarter to the bus driver saying, "You gave me too much change."

"Yes, I know I did," said the driver. "I heard you preach last Sunday on honesty. I thought I would try you out." Had the minister not counted his change, his motives would have been impugned and his character marred. It is tough to carry out the admonition: "To act from honest motives purely."

It may be easy to succumb to selfish wishes and impure motives to achieve a desired object. To men who wished to be empowered to negotiate reward for promises of influence in the Chicago Convention of 1860, Mr. Lincoln replied:

"No, gentlemen, I have not asked for the nomination, and I will not now buy it with pledges. If I am nominated and elected, I shall not go into the presidency as the tool of this man or that man, or as the property of any factor or clique."[1] He was tempted, but stood tall. He acted from honest motives.

Compromise is frequently a part of our dealings with purity of action. There is in the Treasury Department a fund known as "The Conscience Fund." It is there so that those who have cheated the government on tax returns might send in money in response to their consciences. It is reported that a letter came to the department with a check for $25.00 enclosed with these words, "If I don't sleep better the next week, I will send in more money." Here is a case of compromising the conscience or not acting from honest motives.

It is good to ask ourselves if we have ever been a principal character in similar actions.

George Washington, the father of our country said, "I hope I shall always possess firmness and virtue enough to maintain what I consider the most enviable of all titles, the character of an honest man."

The character of an honest person is not formed by being one person now and another later on. Integrity establishes consistency.

Marcus Aurelius gave good advice when he said, "Never esteem anything as of advantage to thee that shall make thee break thy word or lose thy self-respect." If a person loses self-respect he has a poor person to live with. If a person can't go out with his head erect, knowing that he has not been deceitful or dishonest with anyone, then he is in poor company. We do have to live with ourselves.

Sir Galahad put it this way:

> My strength is as the strength of ten,
> Because my heart is pure.

Jesus said it another way, "Blessed are the pure in heart: for they shall see God" (Matt. 5:8). Purity of heart is equal to strength of heart. Impurity of heart draws a veil between the creature and the Creator. Impurity is like leaven; it can permeate the whole person.

Give to yourself, therefore, pure thoughts, honest motives, and proper actions.

There has been much dishonesty in national life, much on the local level, and much in the educational world. Somehow we need to establish confidence in each other so that our word is as good as our bond.

Even though you may or may not be under an honor system, or honor code, I would strongly suggest that you impose one upon yourself that is stronger than any corporate code or system. You are, in this respect, both the doctor and the patient. Don't be careless at this point. Don't be careless at any point because there are some unseen problems that could frustrate you as you meet the challenge.

Note

1. A. K. McClure, ed., *Lincoln's Own Yarns and Stories* (Chicago-Philadelphia: The John C. Winston Company, p. 216.

15

To Trust in God and Heaven Securely

As you meet the challenge of each day, you have an invitation from the Creator of life to live life to the fullest. Your invitation is just as important as any engraved invitation with the letters RSVP (*répondez s' il vous plaît*—reply, if you please) at the bottom. Your response, I hope, will be, I will trust in God and heaven. There could be no better one.

You have a right to want assurance of God's companionship, and you also have a right to want no guess for a dying pillow.

Recently George MacIntyre, football coach of the Vanderbilt University Commodores who was selected Coach of the Year of his conference and National Coach of the Year, was asked by his pastor to give his testimony on a Sunday morning after the biggest game, and closing one, of the regular season. He stated that two years before his team had lost by a score of sixty-six to seven, and that was indeed a low moment. Then he told of the twenty-eight to twenty-one victory the day before over their arch rival, bringing to a close one of the most successful seasons in the university's history and bringing also a bowl bid. Coach MacIntyre said that he was able to maintain some sense of equanimity between the low moment and the high moment by his strong faith in God and his devotion to Christ his Savior. What a testimony! What a response to life! What faith!

But Coach MacIntyre's faith was not without foundation. The twenty-third Psalm says, "He leadeth me beside the still waters. He restoreth my soul" (v. 2-3). Proverbs 3:5-6 is further proof of the validity of his faith, "Trust in the Lord with all thine heart;

and lean not unto thine own understanding. In all thy ways acknowledge him, and he shall direct thy paths."

Jesus spent much of his time directing the minds of those who heard him to place implicit trust in him and the Holy Spirit. He told his disciples that he would ask his Father to send another Comforter—the Paraclete, or one alongside, even the Spirit of truth—who would guide them into all truth (John 14:16; 16:7). The Comforter or the Holy Spirit would not be subject to arrest by the world and would become their guide, advocate, and companion. That Spirit is as available today as he was then.

I can almost hear you say, "Oh, this all sounds so good, so simple, but it is not that easy. Life is often awesome, fearsome." You are right but you must exercise your faith, flex your faith muscles. God's Word is not false. The psalmist expressed it this way, "What time I am afraid, I will trust in thee" (56:3).

You further add, "But God makes demands upon me before all of these good-sounding promises come true." Right you are again. But the trade-off is greatly to your advantage. God does make promises to you, make demands of you, but he also helps you claim his promises and fulfill his demands. The prophet Micah asked, "What doth the Lord require of thee, but to do justly, and to love mercy, and to walk humbly with thy God" (Mic. 6:8)? Christ put his demands in these words, "If any man will come after me, let him deny himself, and take up his cross, and follow me" (Matt. 16:24). What a challenge!

Jenny, our granddaughter, when three and a half years of age, was in the kitchen with her father. Somehow she got a paring knife. Fearing she might cut herself, her father asked for the knife. She gave it to him but said, "If I cut myself, God will heal me, won't he?" That's a tough question to answer for a child so young. However, her father, with endless patience, tried to explain that God doesn't function that way. He does not stand by to heal us automatically when accidentally or in carelessness we cut or injure ourselves. After the lengthy explanation, she replied, "Well if that is the case I think I will get me another God." Touché but don't write it off as childhood chatter. Many young people take the same stance; "If God won't do it my way, play the game my way, then I will leave him and go another way to another less demanding."

My sincerest plea to you is that you refrain from taking such a position. You can't find another god like the one and only God.

I am purposely making this the briefest of all the chapters, not because it is the least significant but because it is the most significant with the hope that you will ponder it slowly and carefully.

About a half century ago the king of England, in addressing his subjects at the close of the year, spoke this message to them over the radio: "And I said to the man who stood at the gate of the year, 'Give me a light that I might tread safely in the unknown.' And he said to me, 'Put your hand into the hand of God, and it shall be to you more than a light and safer than a known way.'" What advice!

Hermann Hagedorn, author of the little book *The Bomb that Fell on America*, imagined that a representative of the American people was standing before God to plead our frightful case and heard the Lord say, "Look again, look deep, and say what you see."

Man replied:

> "I talked about love, but I myself never loved."
> "What else?"
> "I talked about Christ, but I worshipped only myself."
> "What else?"
> "I talked about truth but I never dared look in her face."

Then the voice came again and said:

> "Give me your life and I will make it a spade to dig
> the foundations of a new world, a crowbar to pry
> loose the rocks, a hoe to mix sand and cement, a
> trowel to bind stone and stone and make them a
> wall.
> Man without God is a bubble in the sea, a single
> grain of sand on an infinite beach.

> God without man is a mind without tongue or ears
>   or eyes or fingers or feet.
> God and man together, We are such power as not
>   all the atoms in all Creation can match!"[1]

Would you, my dear reader, put your hand into the hand of God? If you would trust in God and heaven securely, hear these words of G. A. Studdert-Kennedy:

> How do I know that God is good? I don't
> I gamble like a man. I bet my life
> Upon one side in life's great war. I must
> I can't stand out. I must take sides. The man
> Who is a neutral in this fight is not
> A man. He's bulk and body without breadth,
> Cold leg of lamb without mint sauce. A fool.
> He makes me sick. Good Lord! Weak tea! Cold slops!
> I want to live, live out, not wobble through
> My life somehow, and then into the dark.
> I must have God.
> . . . .
> Well—God's my leader, and I hold that He
> Is good, and strong enough to work His plan
> And purpose out to its appointed end.
> . . . .
> For God is love. Such is my Faith, and such
> My reasons for it, and I find them strong
> Enough. And You? You want to argue? Well,
> I can't. It is a choice. I choose the Christ.[2]

Thanks for allowing me to come along. You can meet the challenge. Choose the Christ! If you choose Christ, you can feel very secure in your trust in God and heaven.

Jesus is quoted by John as saying:

"Let not your heart be troubled [afraid, worried, or doubtful]: ye believe in God, believe also in me. In my Father's house are many mansions: if it were not so, I would have told you. I go to prepare a place for you. And if I go and prepare a place for you, I will come again, and receive you unto myself; that where I am, there ye may be also" (John 14:1-3).

It is not recorded that Jesus ever said at any other time "if it were not so." The strong and correct inference is that he wanted no doubt in his followers' minds. He can be trusted! Take him at his word. There is no better friend.

Invite him to accompany you as you meet the challenges of life. He is a wise, compassionate Companion who has strength and skill to assist you when needed. He will not go, however, if you don't invite him.

Ask him today!

Notes

1. Hermann Hagedorn, *The Bomb that Fell on America* (New York: Association Press, 1950), pp. 50-52.
2. G.A. Studdert-Kennedy in *The Best of G.A. Studdert-Kennedy* compiled by a friend (New York: Harper and Brothers, 1948), pp. 147-149.

Herbert C. Gabhart

Herbert C. Gabhart is chancellor of Belmont College, Nashville, Tennessee. For twenty-three years he served as president of Belmont College. Dr. Gabhart has served in leadership roles in higher education, in civic organizations, and in the Tennessee Baptist Convention and the Southern Baptist Convention. He was educated at Carson-Newman College (B.S.), Bowling Green, Kentucky, Business College, The Southern Baptist Theological Seminary, and the President's Institute, Harvard University.